The BUTT HELLO

and other ways my cats drive me crazy

written and illustrated
by ted meyer

art direction
amy inouye

Published by:

Santa Monica Press LLC
P.O. Box 1076
Santa Monica, CA 90406-1076
1-800-784-9553
www.santamonicapress.com
books@santamonicapress.com

Printed in China

Santa Monica Press books are available at special quantity discounts when purchased in bulk by corporations, organizations, or groups. Please call our Special Sales department at 1-800-784-9553.

Library of Congress Cataloging-in-Publication Data

Meyer, Ted.
The butt hello : and other ways my cats drive me crazy / written & illustrated by Ted Meyer.
p. cm.

ISBN 1-891661-25-6
1. Cats--Humor. I. Title.

PN6231.C23 M49 2002
741.5'973--dc21

2002017602

With apologies to
Steven & Steven.

They start out

PETITE and playful.

LARGE They end up and lazy.

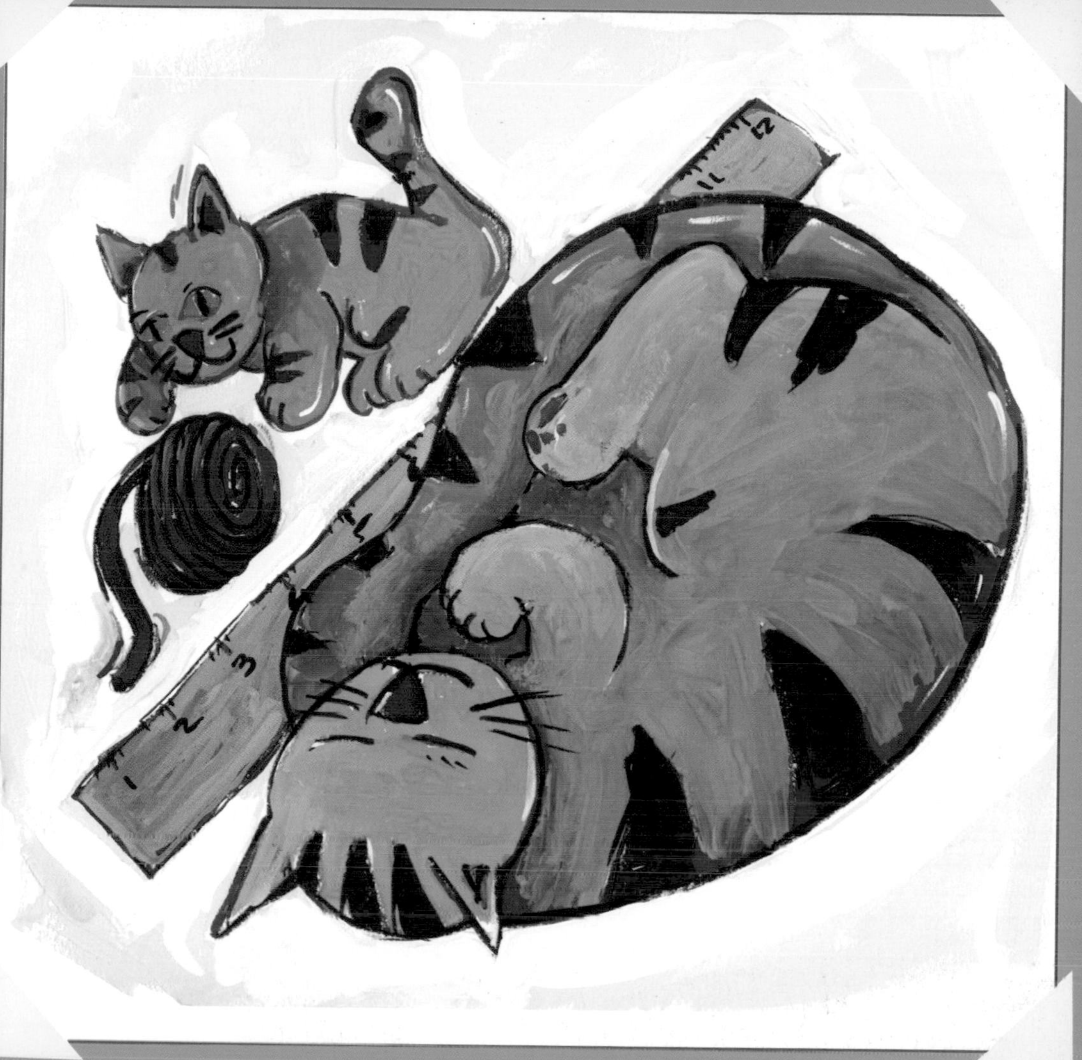

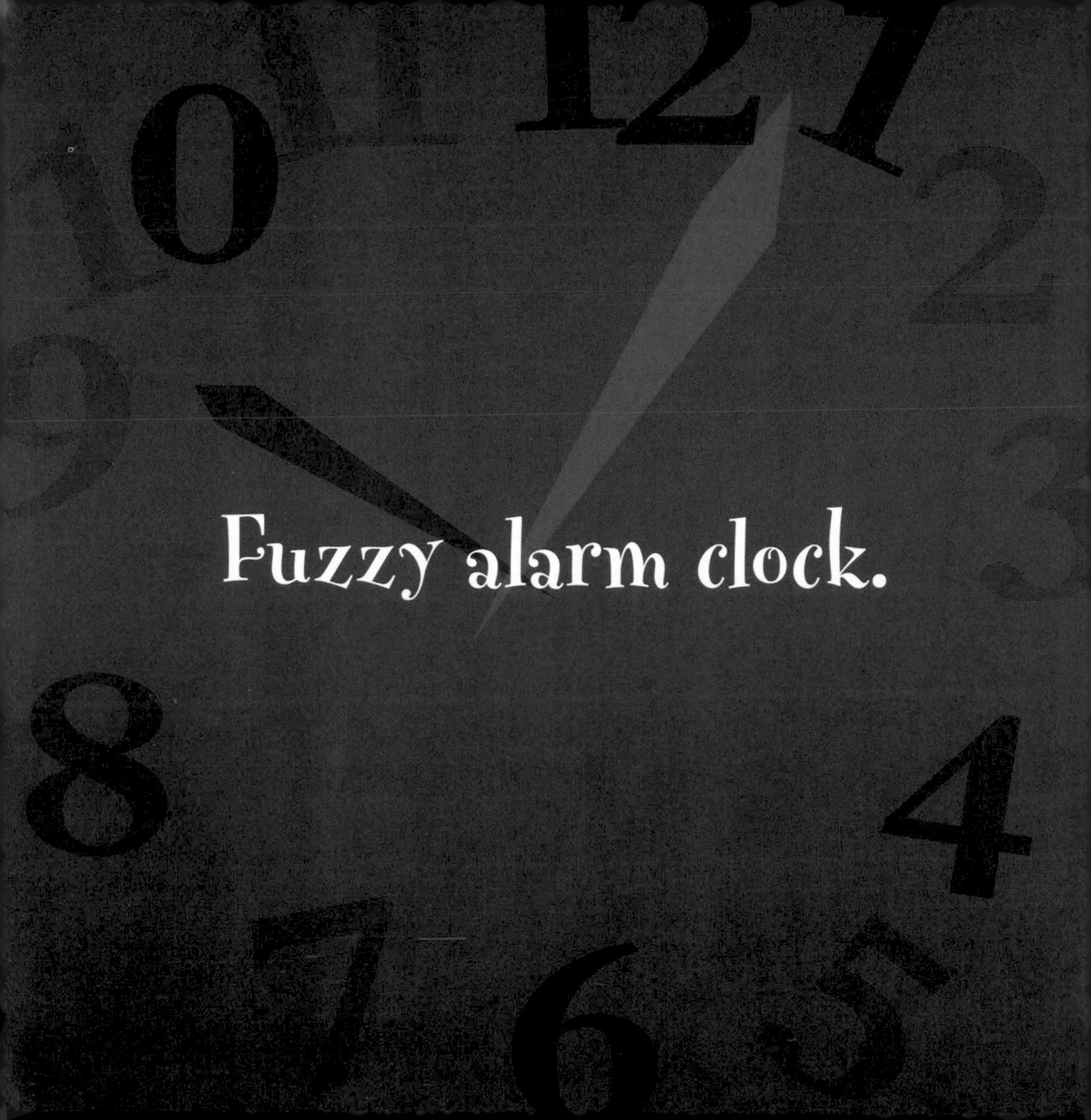

Fuzzy alarm clock.

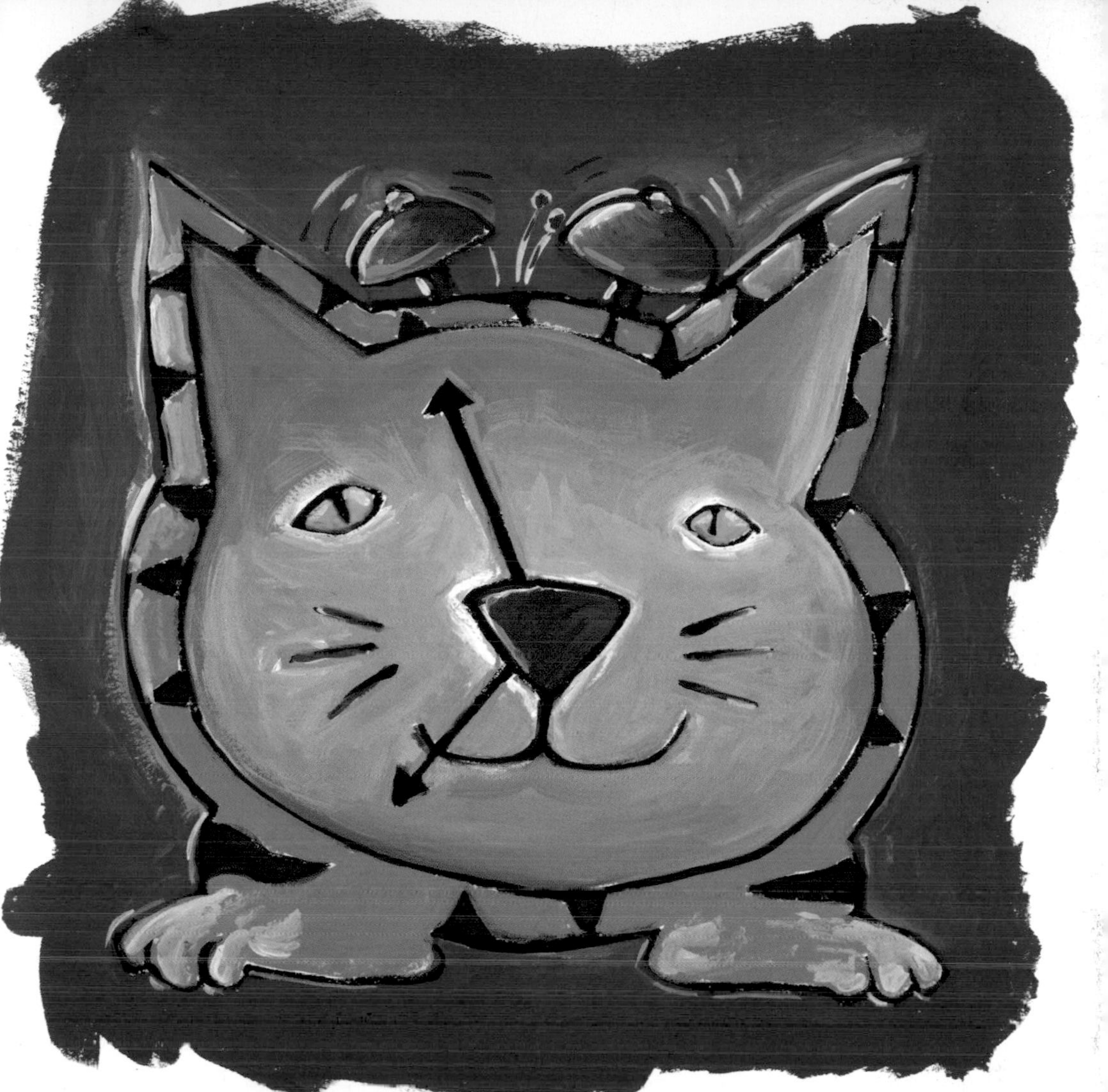

They have brains
the size
of a walnut.

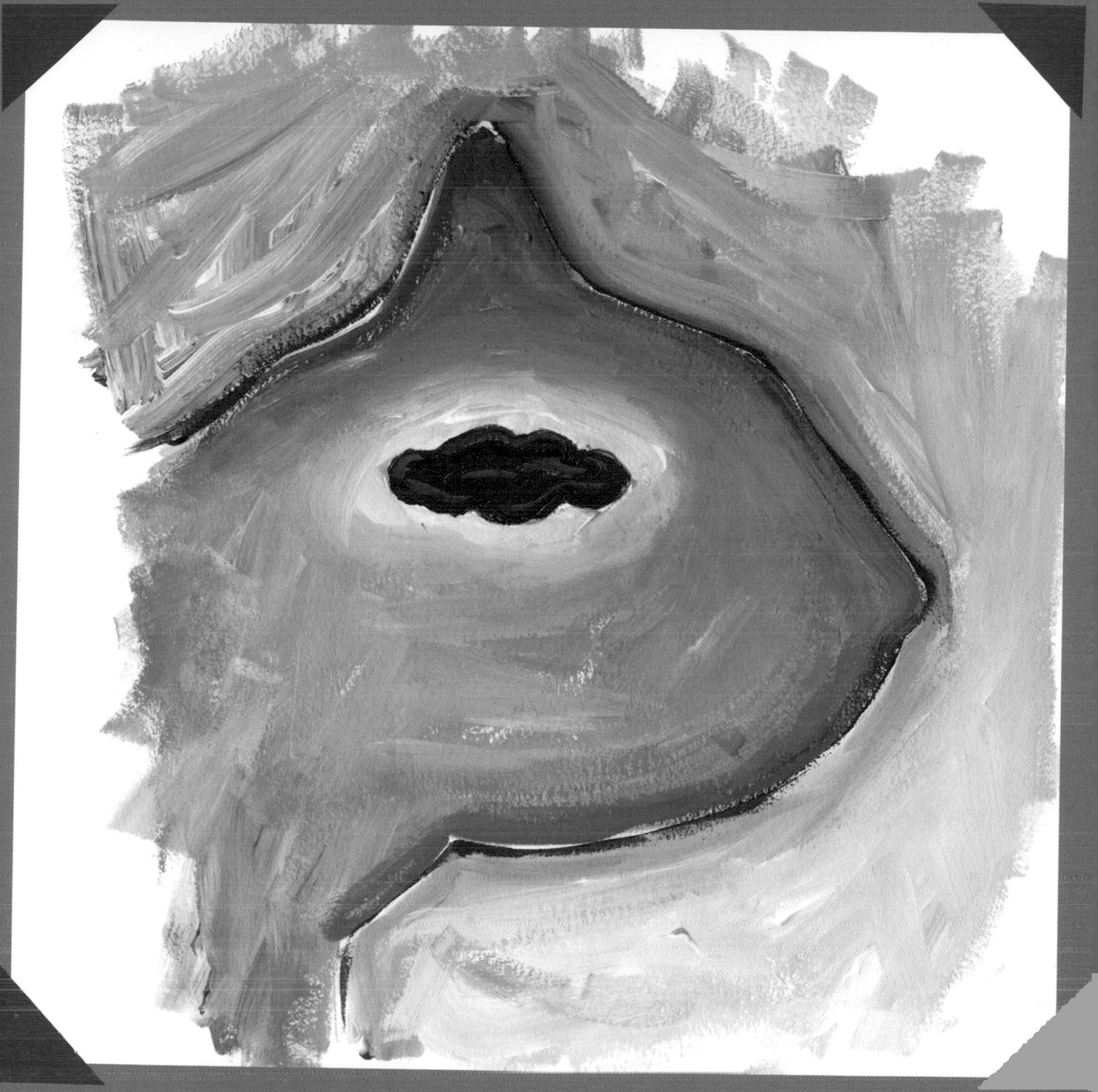

They sleep **ALL** day.

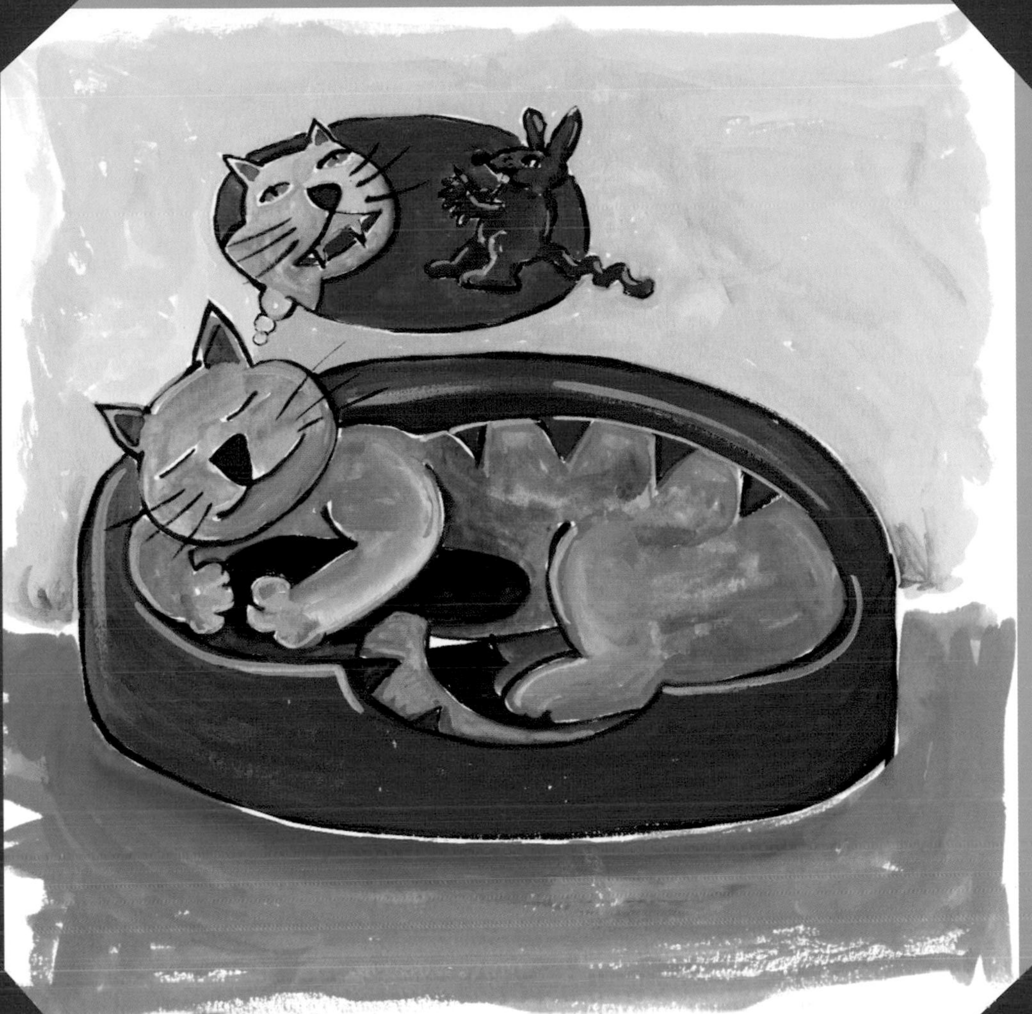

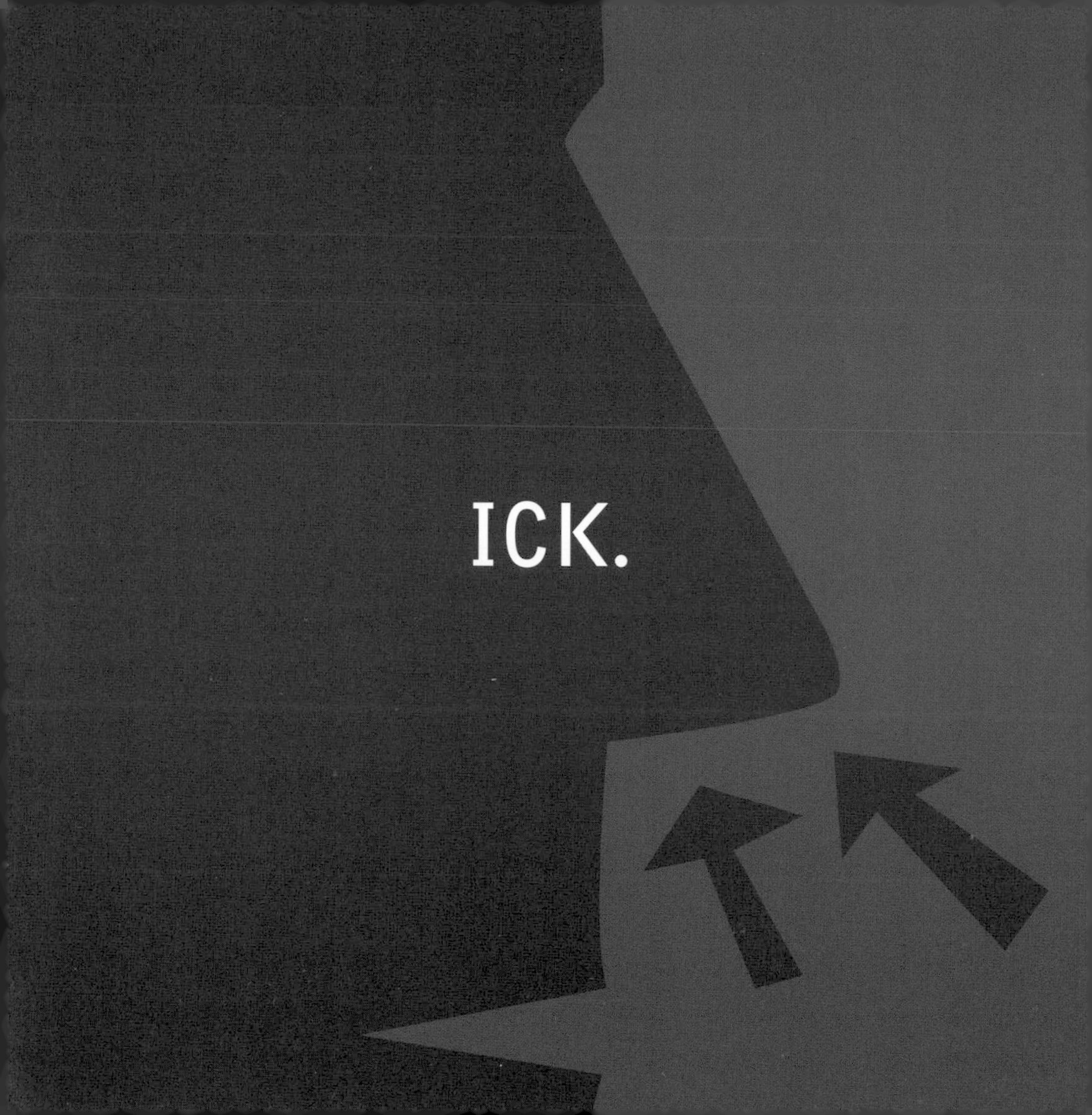
ICK.

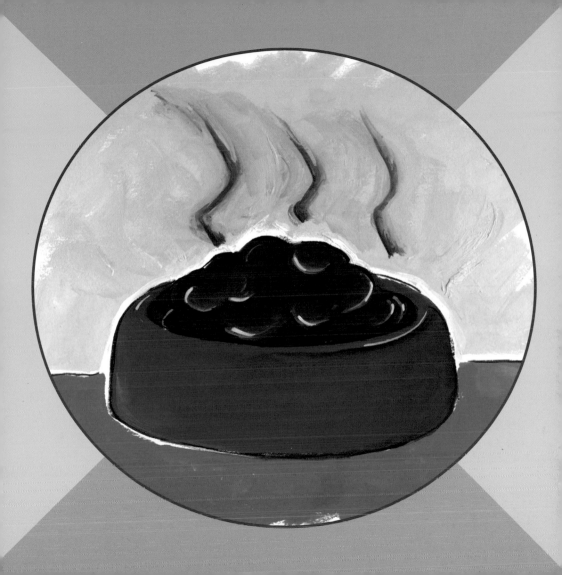

They eat mouse heads.

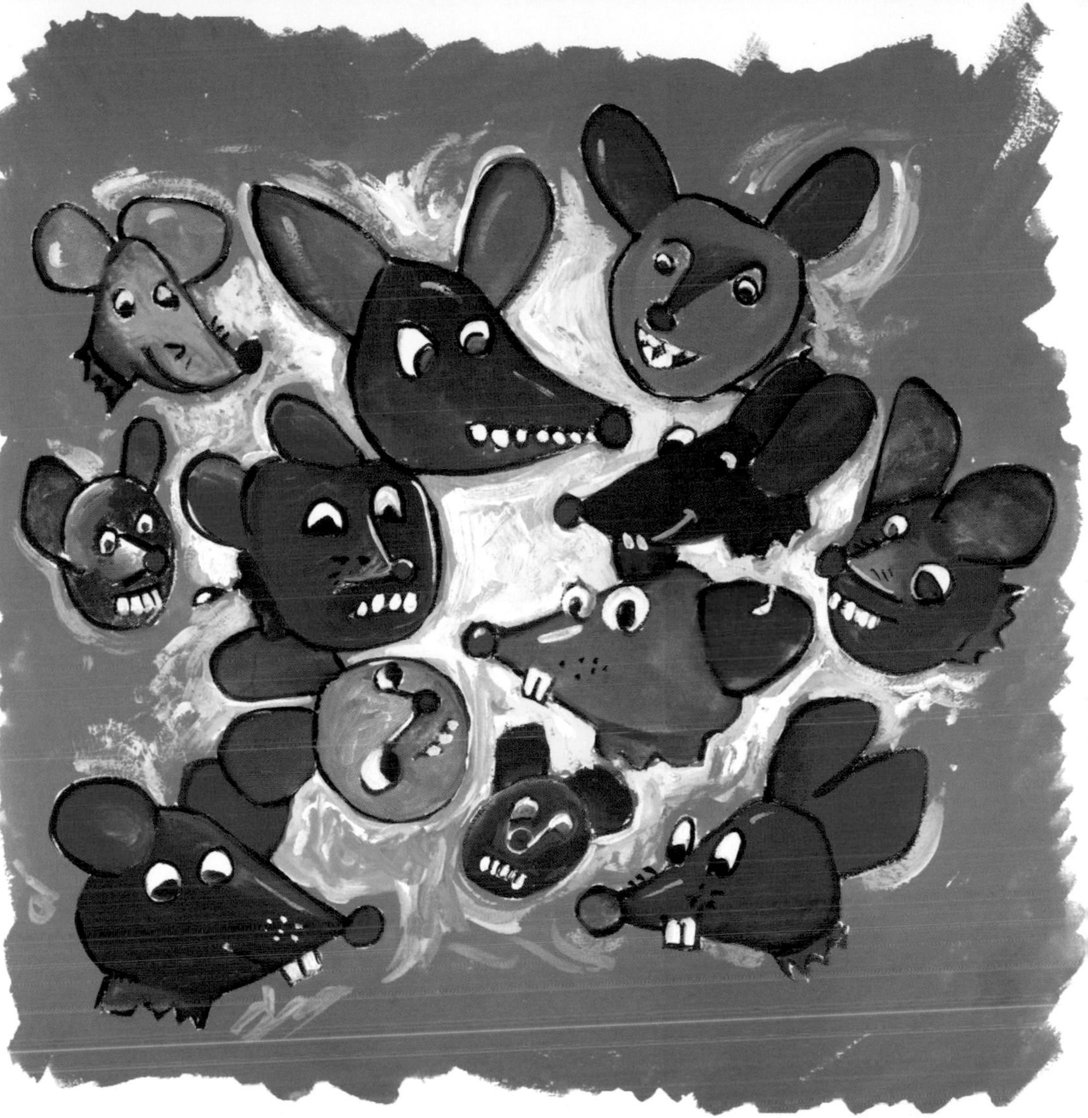

Midnight.

Toe attack.

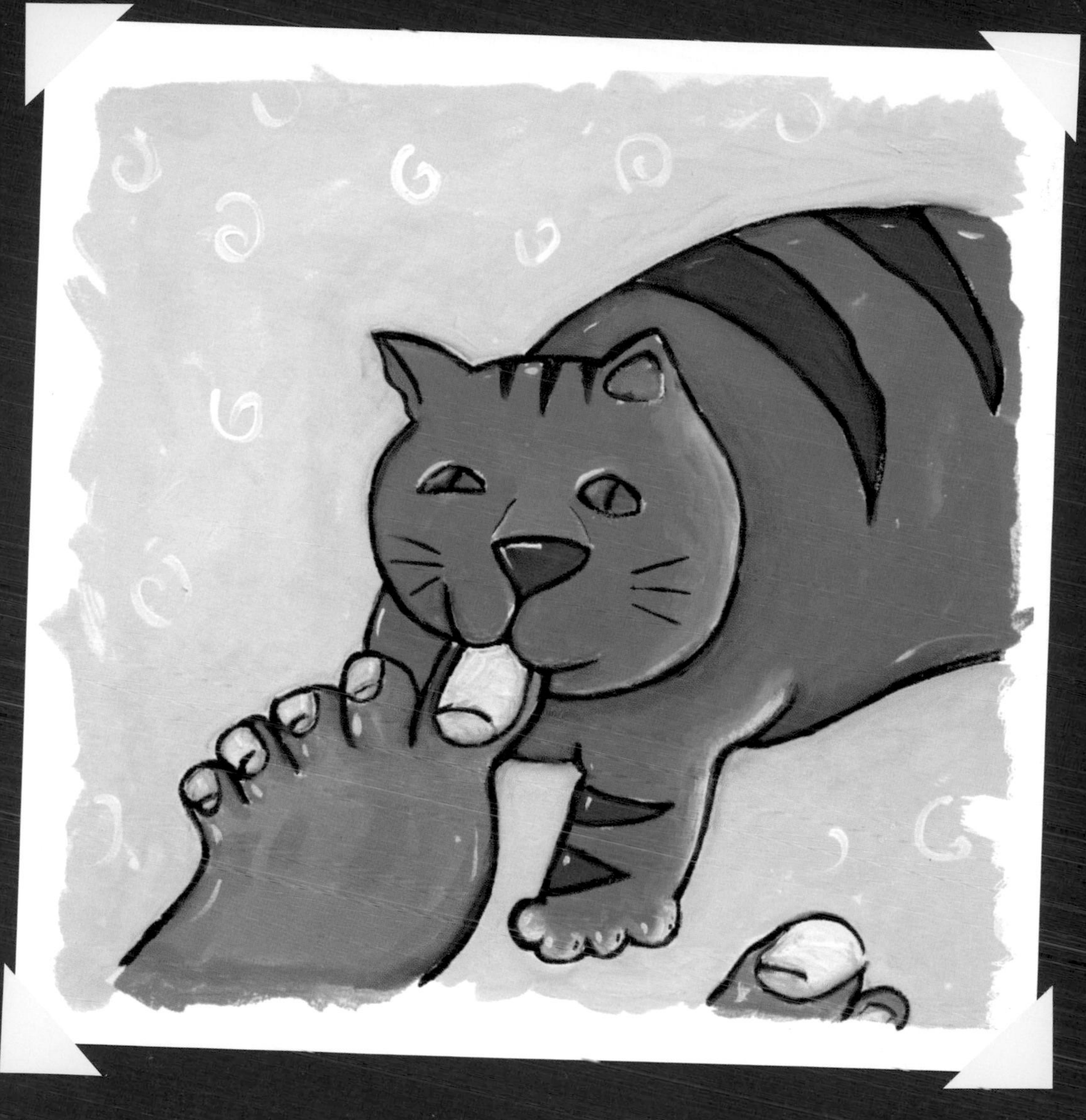

They're sneaky.

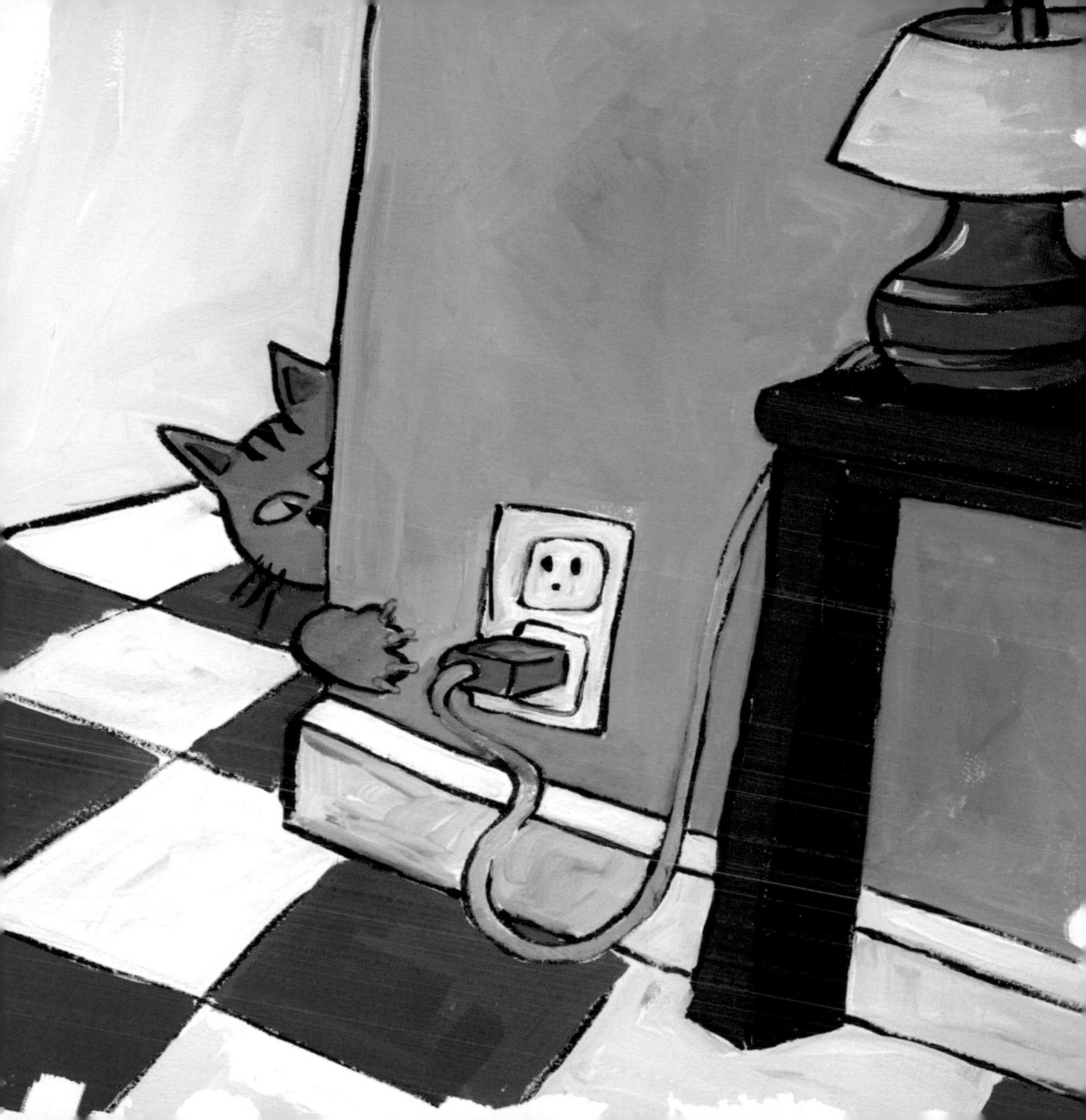

Cat hairs
all over
my favorite
shirt
pants
jacket
coat
socks
sweater

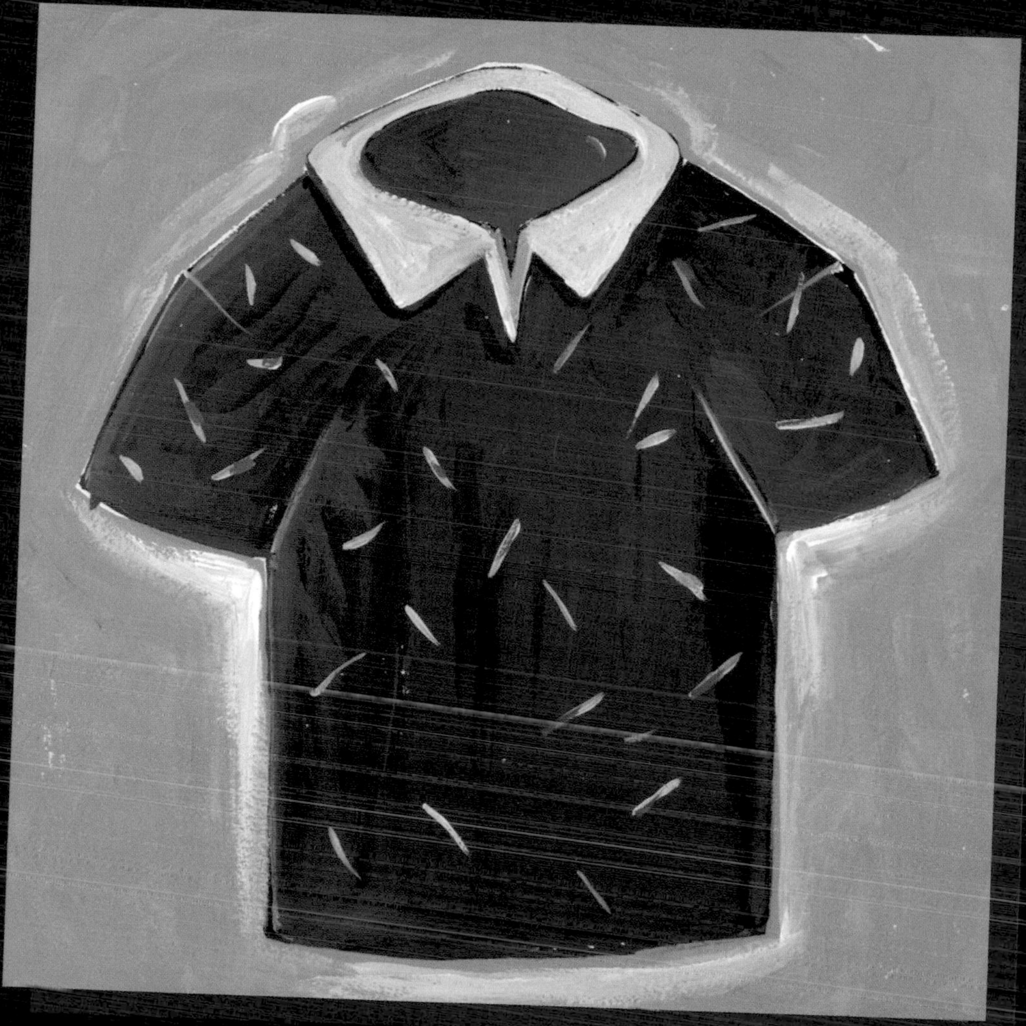

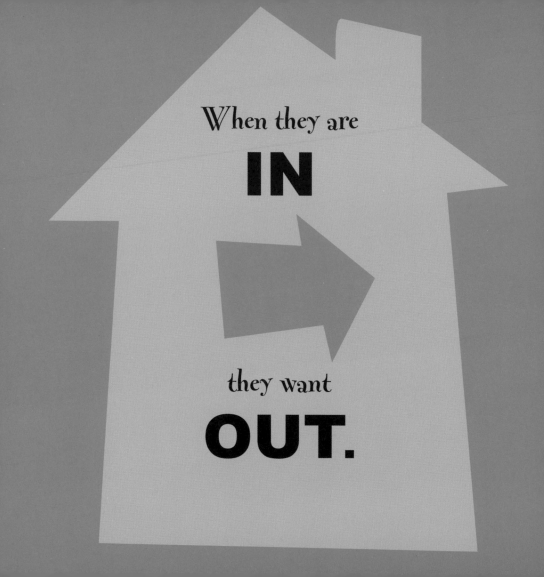

When they are

IN

they want

OUT.

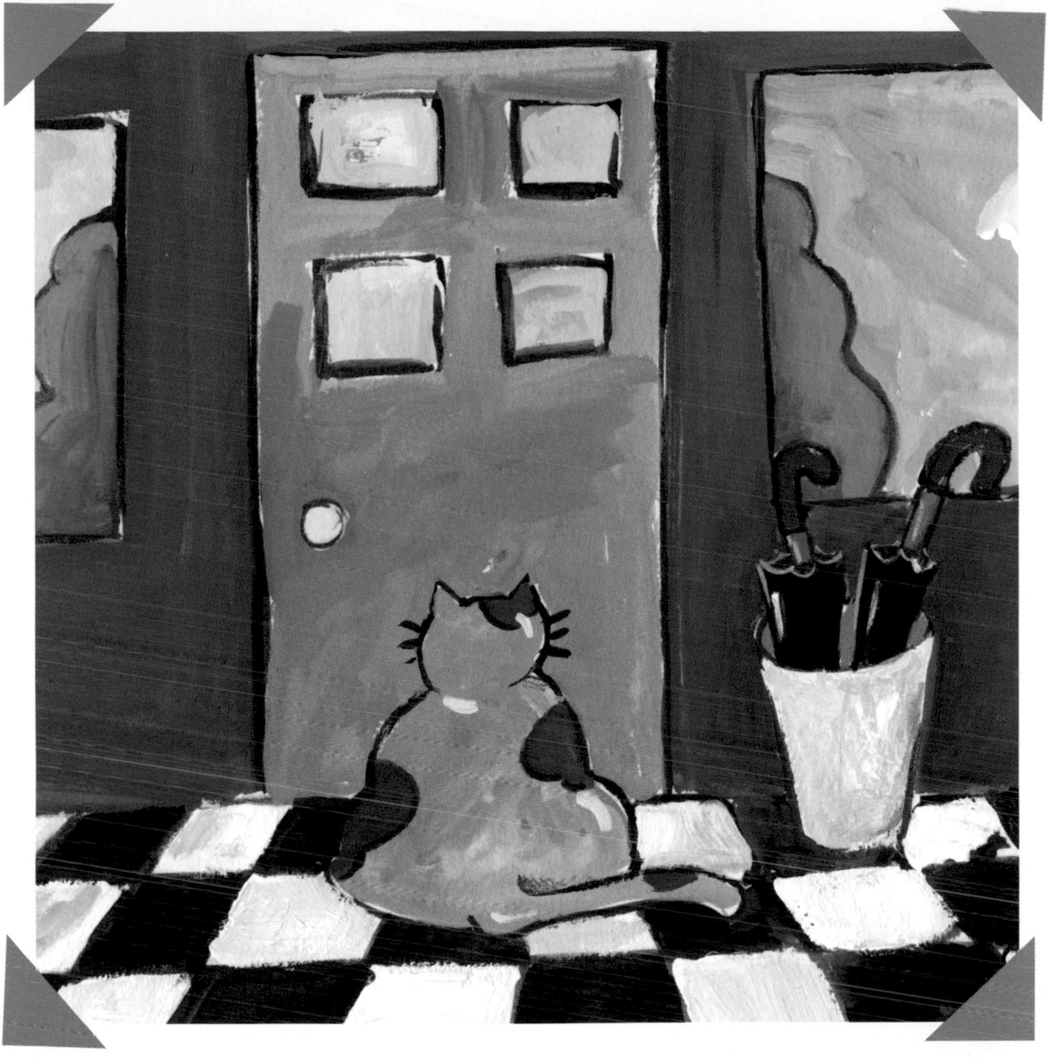

When they are

OUT

they want

IN.

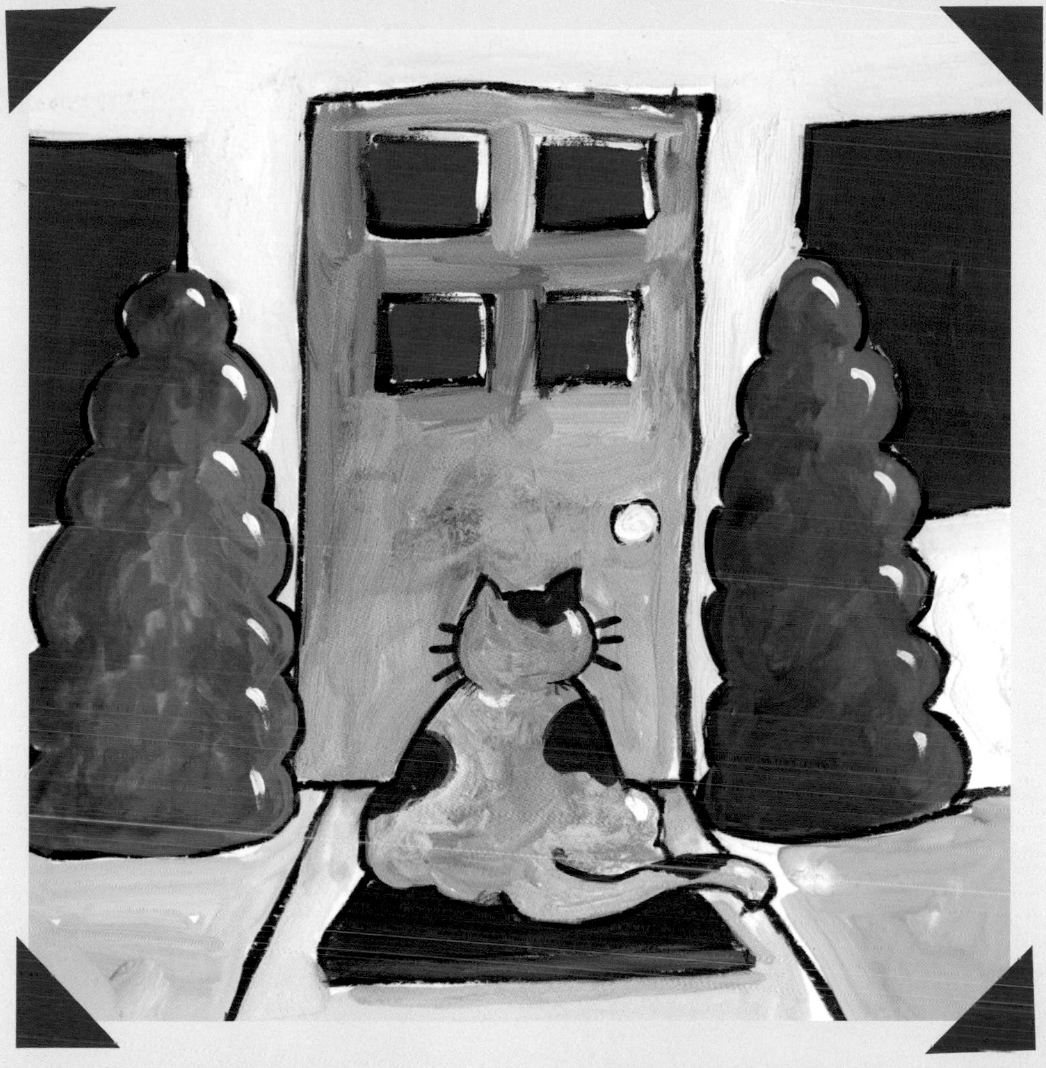

The Butt Hello.

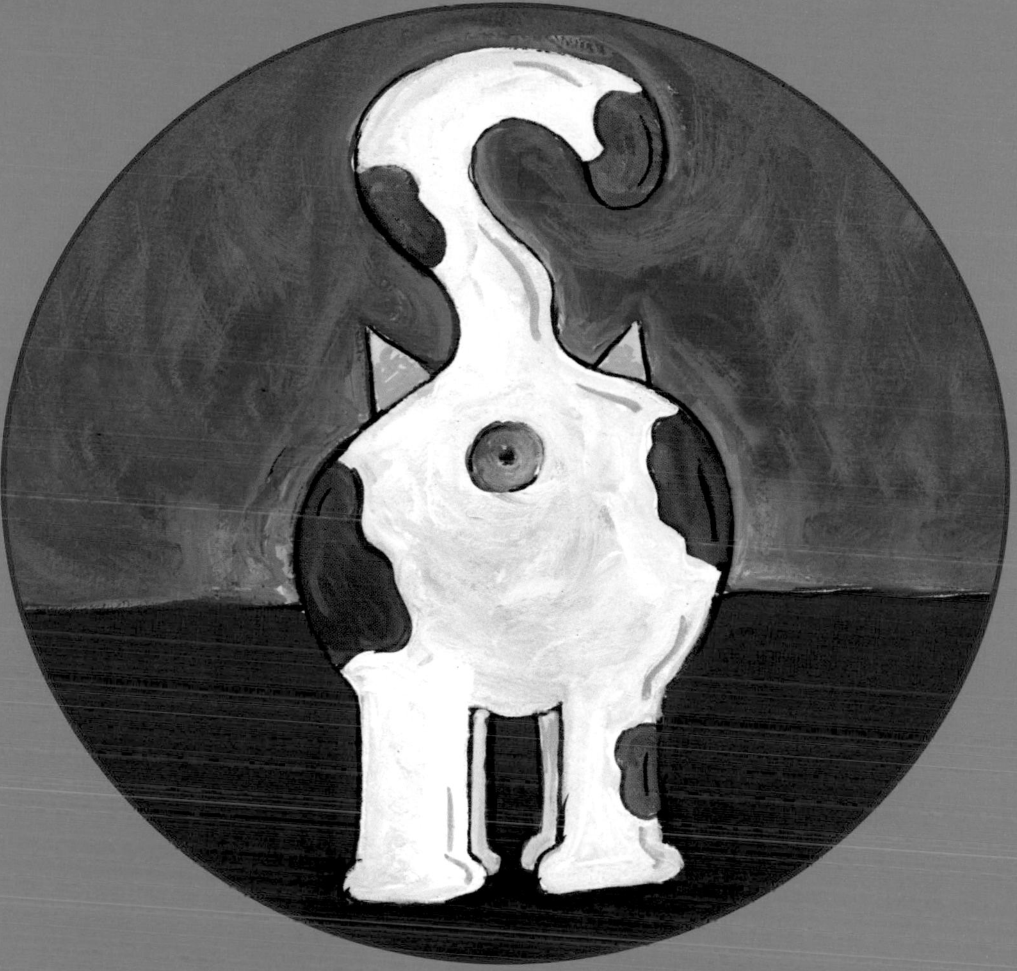

Fishy tuna breath.

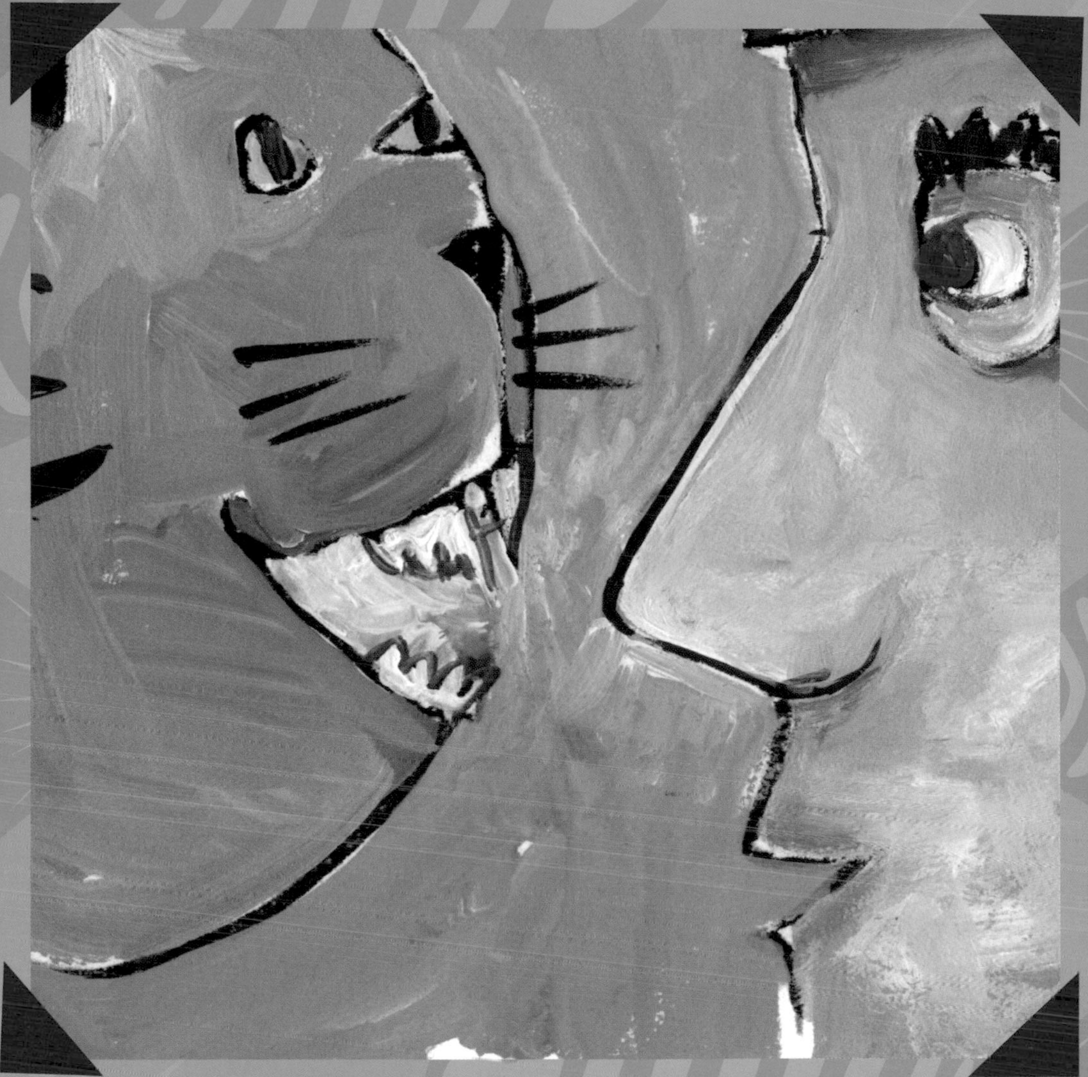

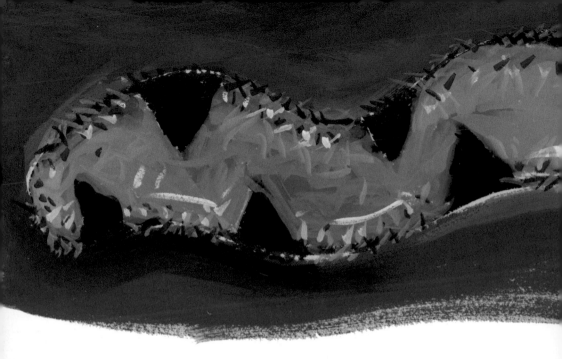

Soft and fluffy.

Sharp and **pointy.**

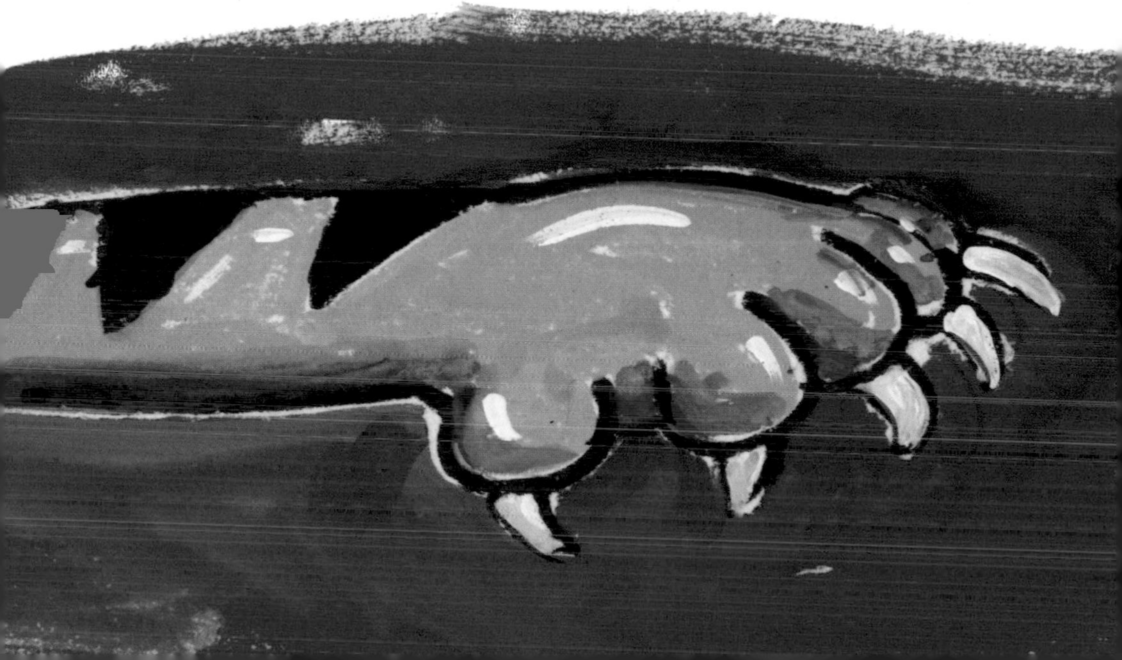

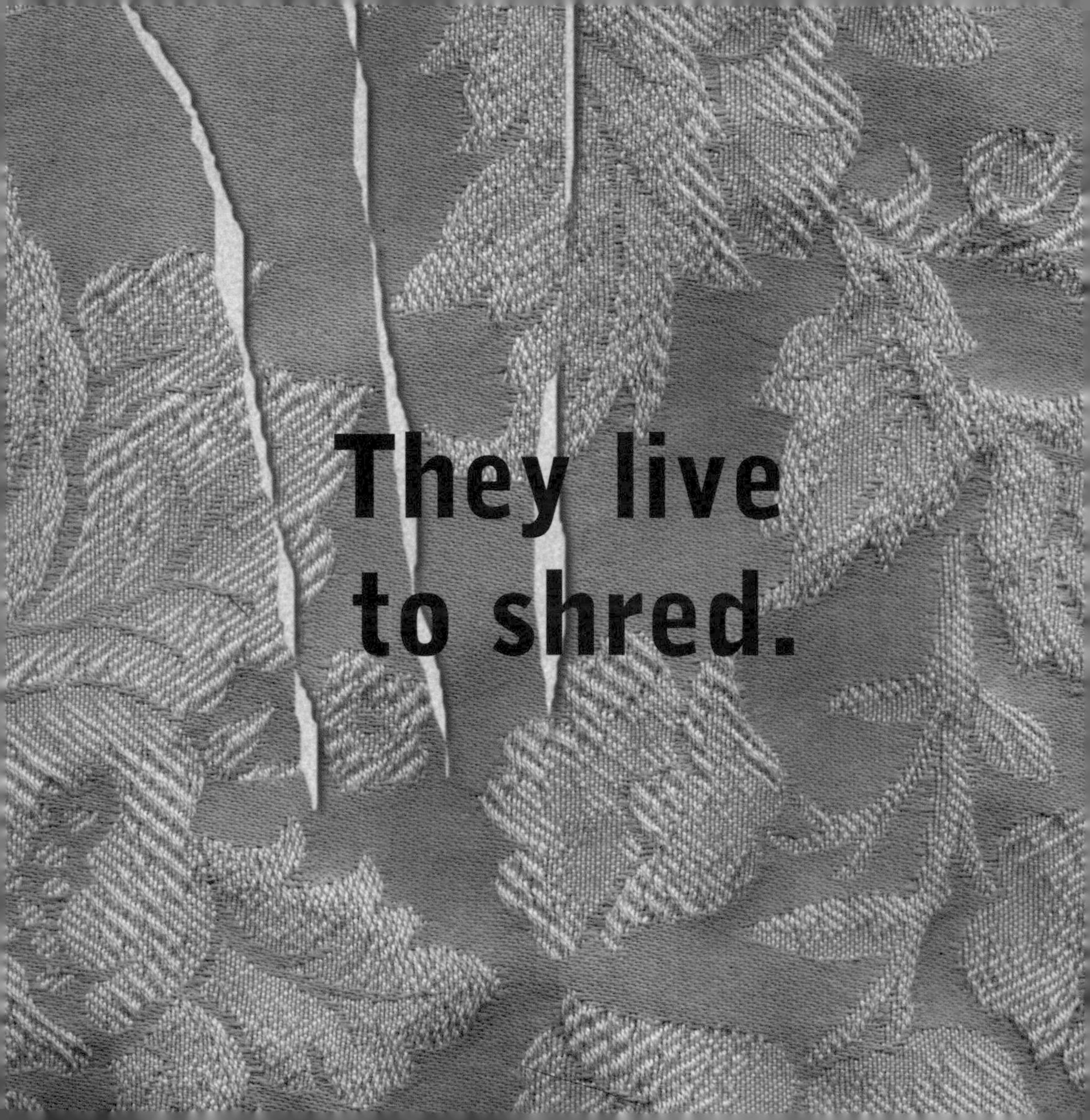
They live
to shred.

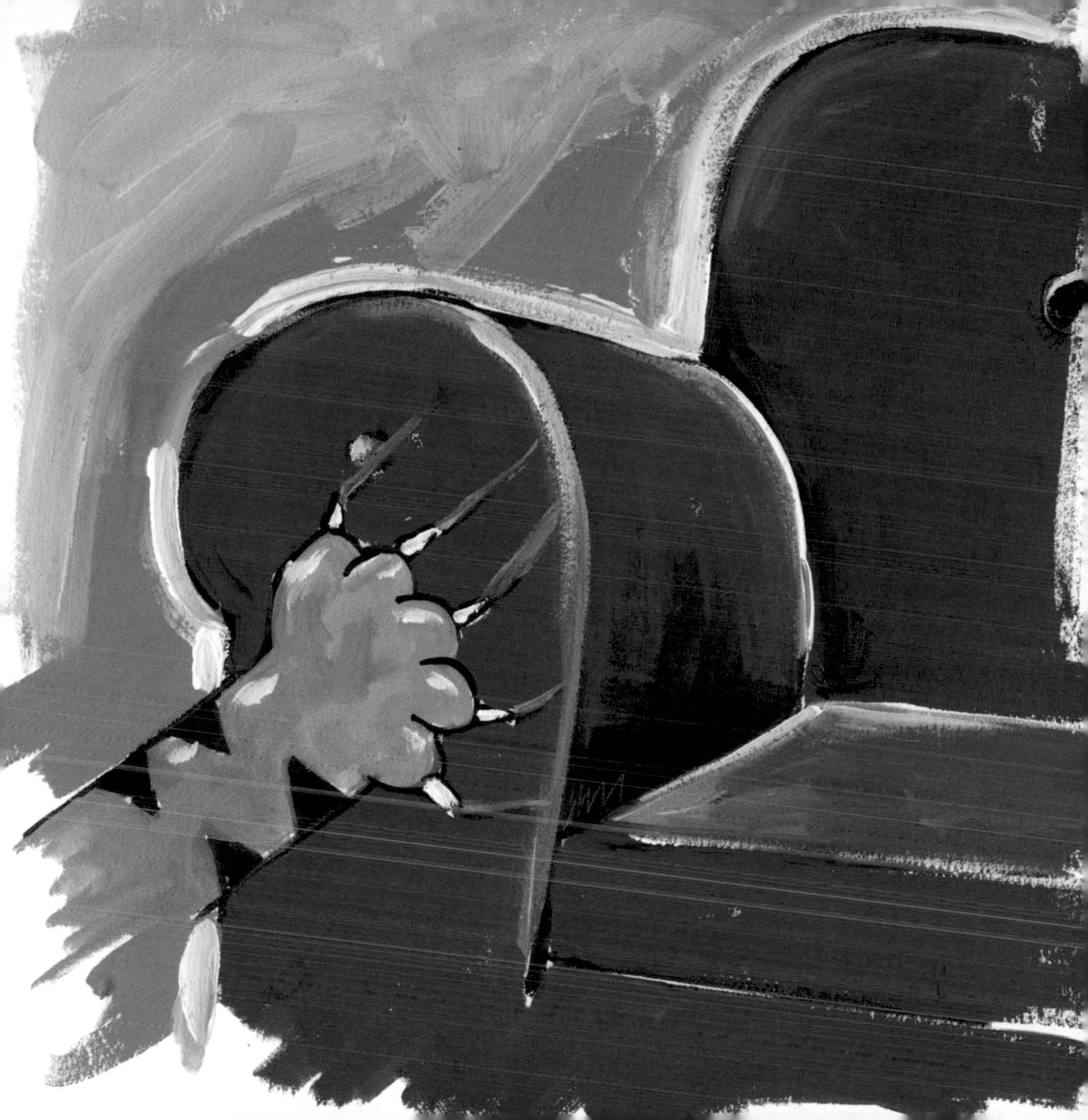

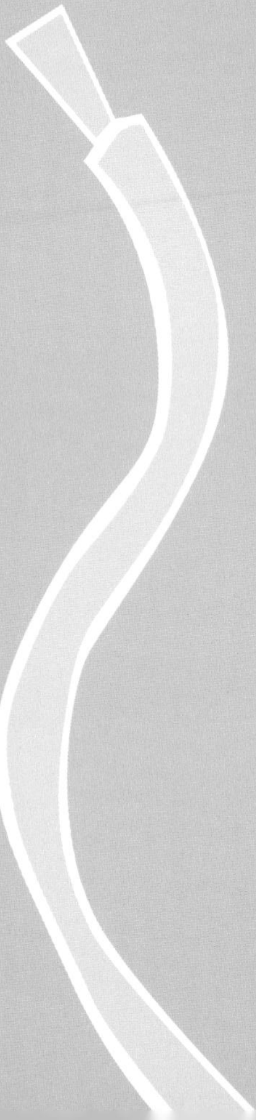

Shoelaces
are not
cat toys.

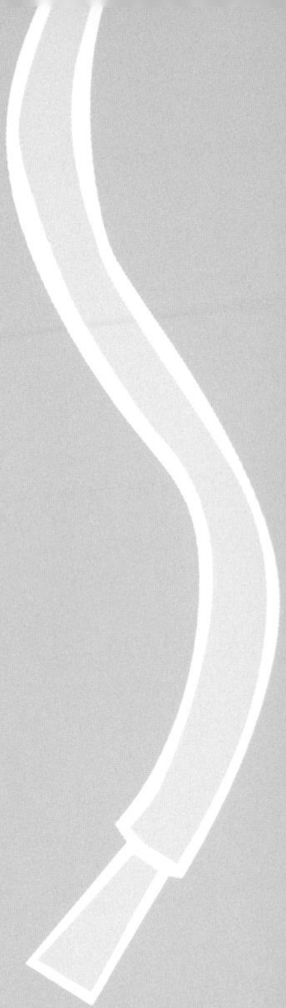

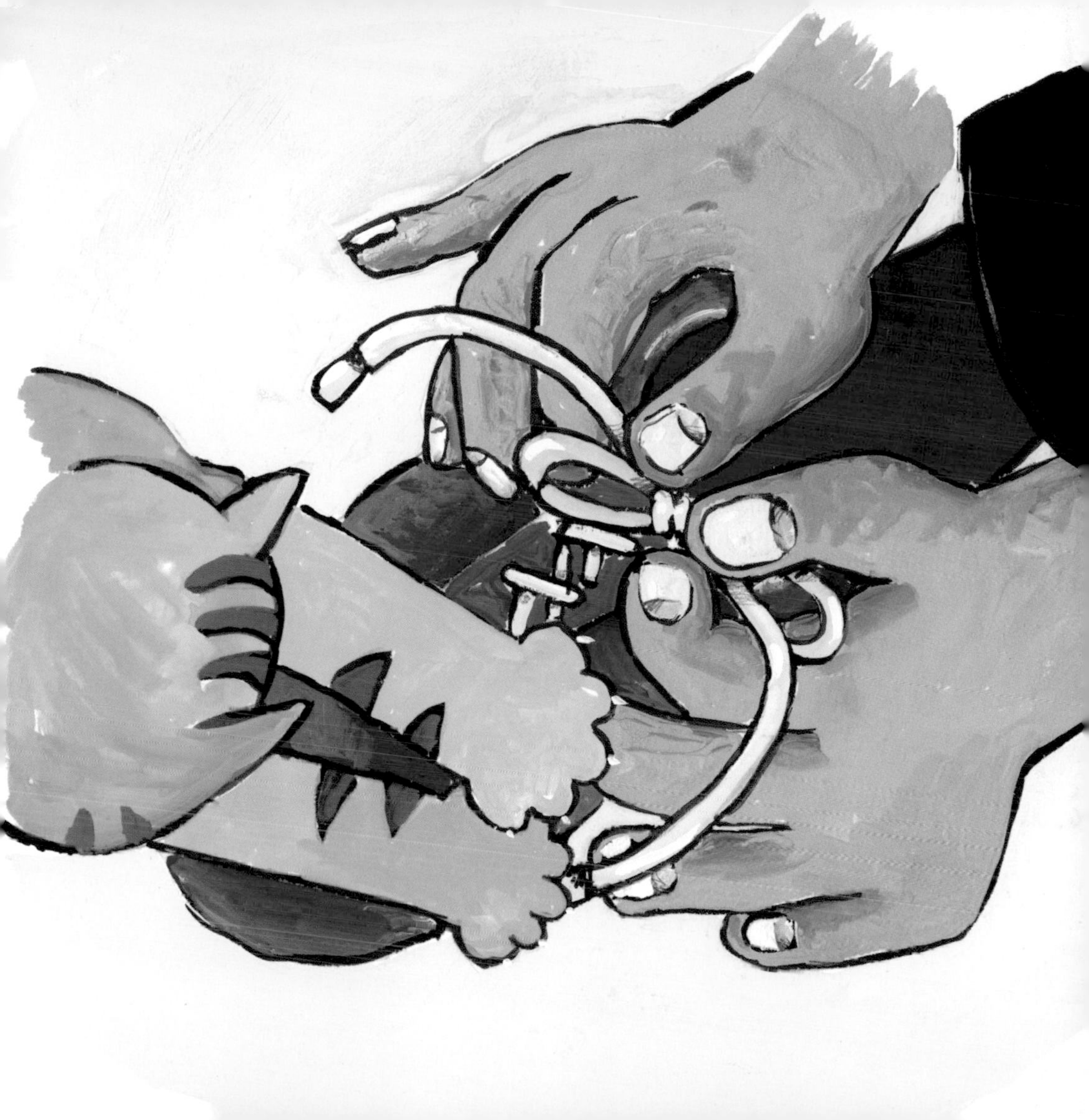

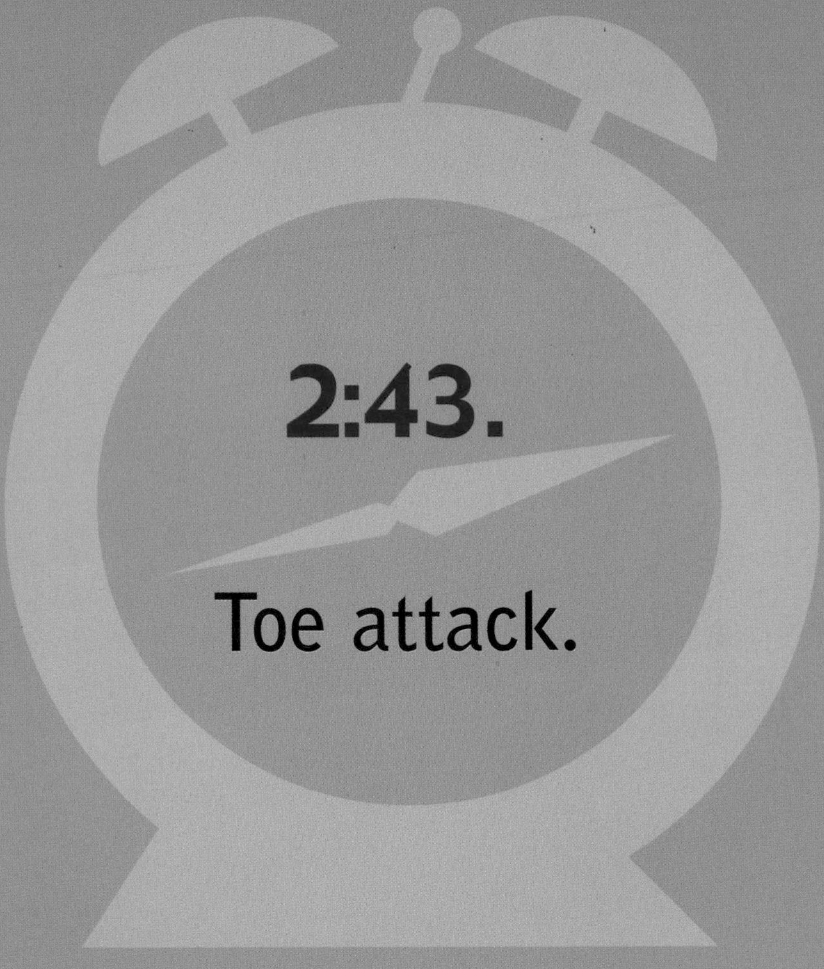
2:43.
Toe attack.

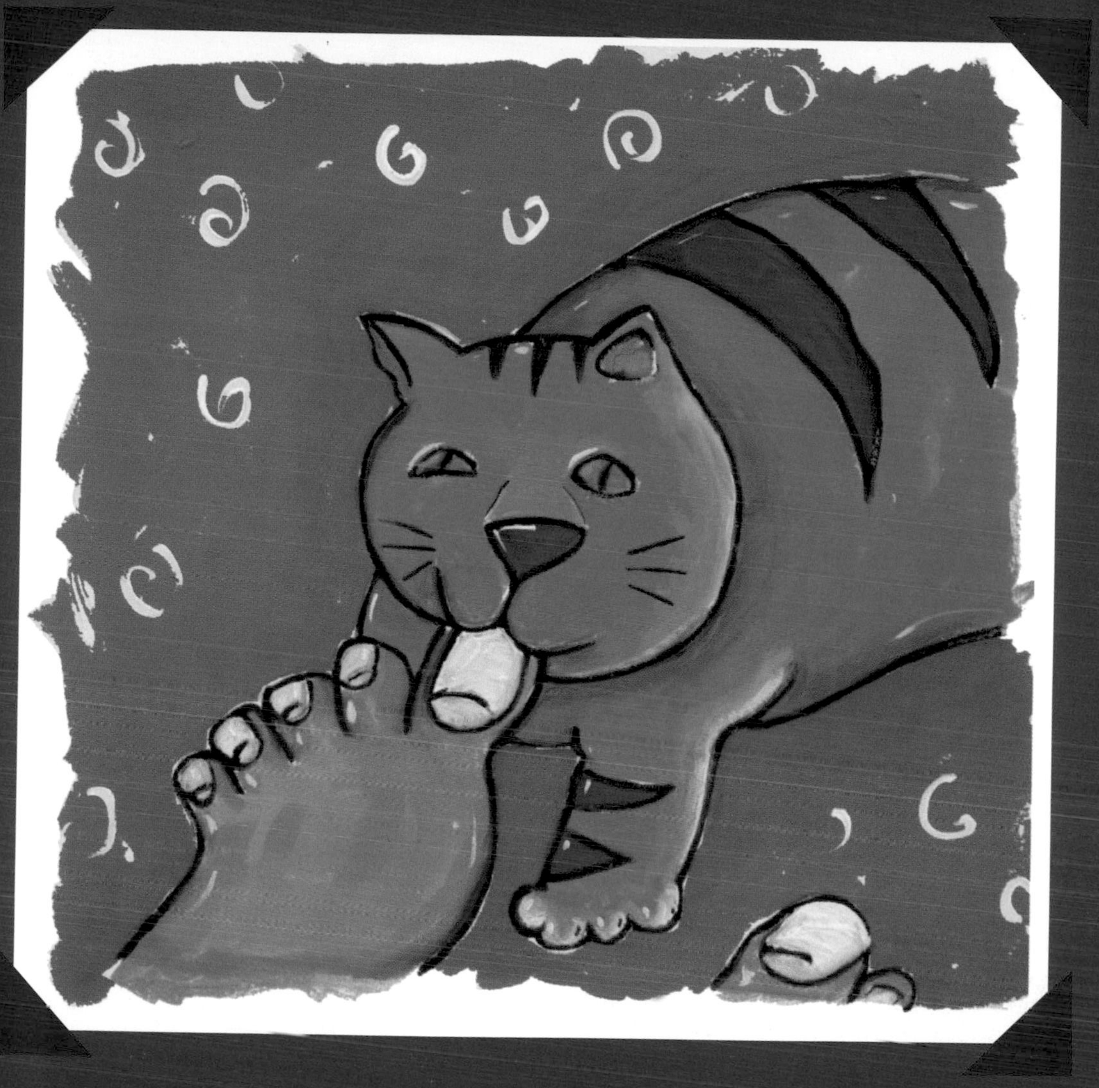

Fleas.

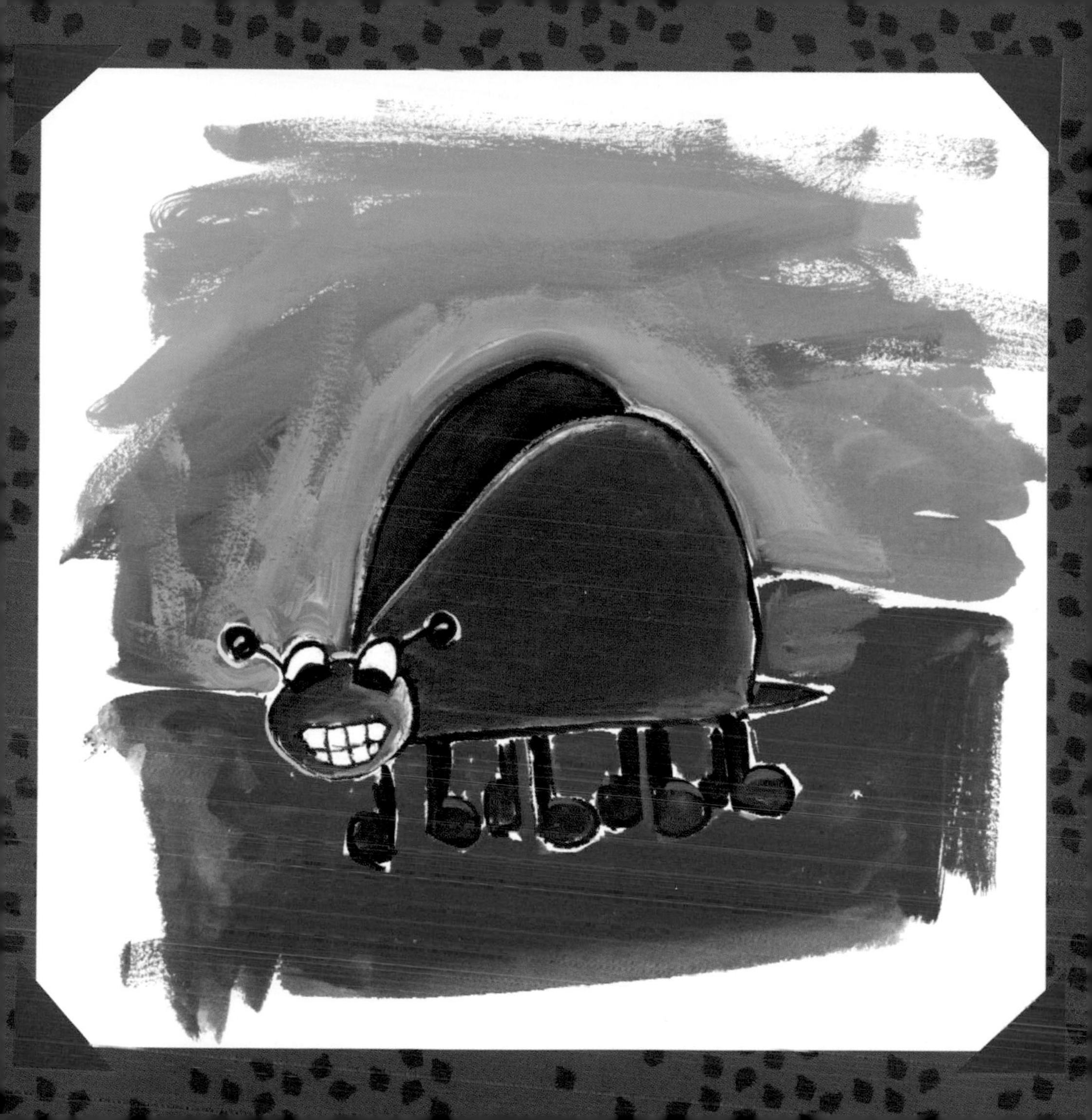

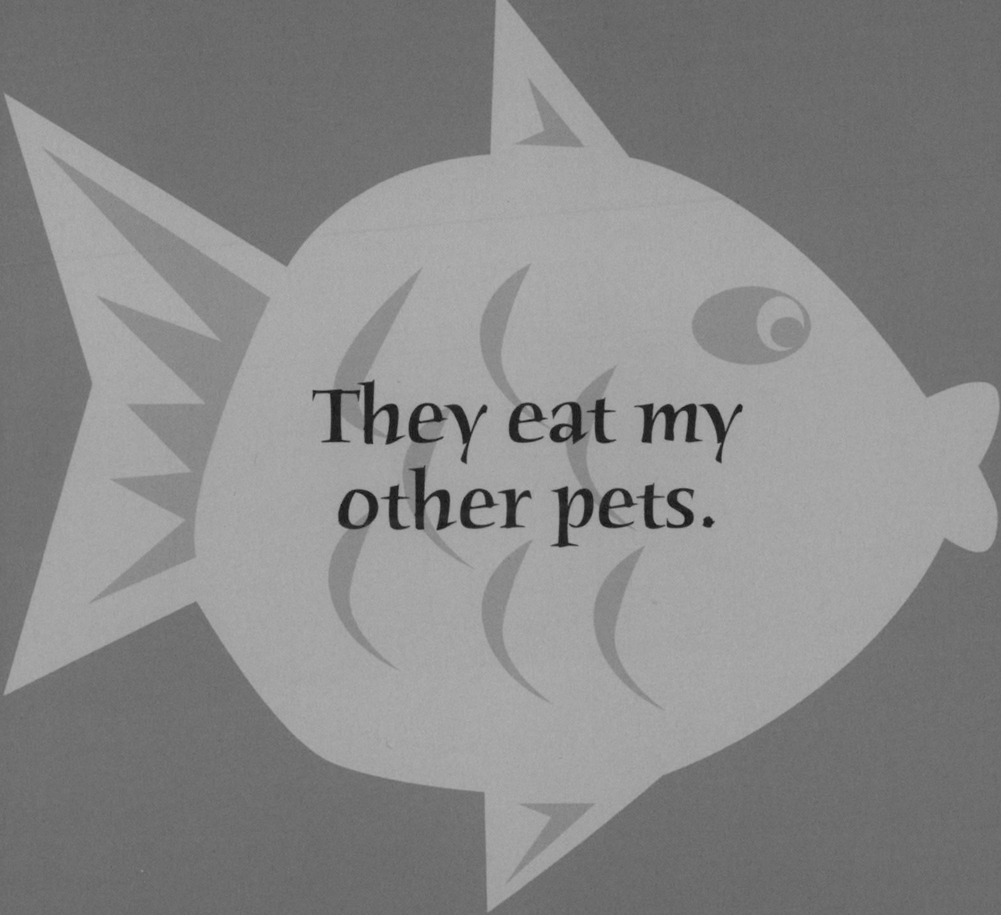

They eat my
other pets.

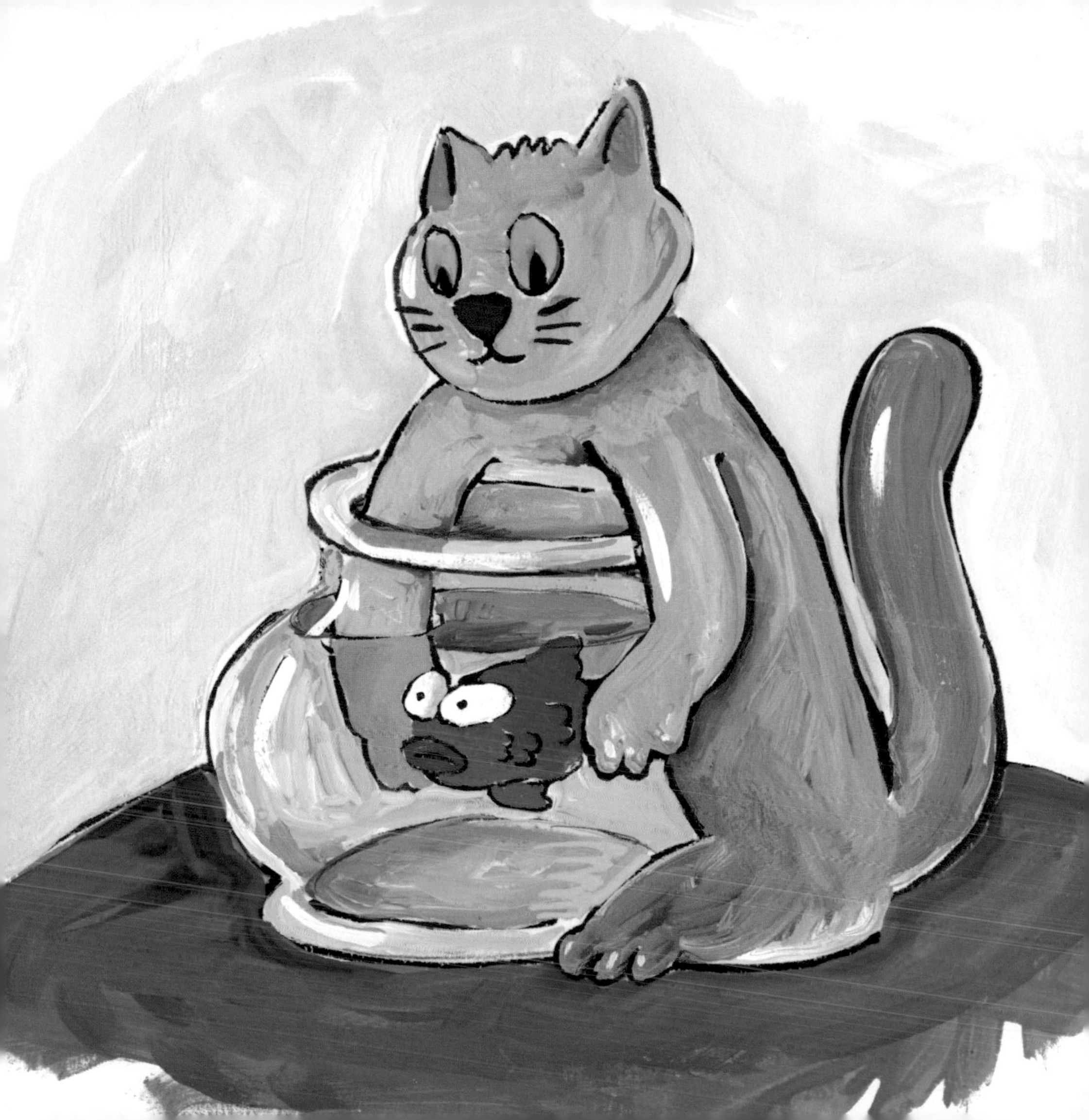

Some cats have
way too many toes.

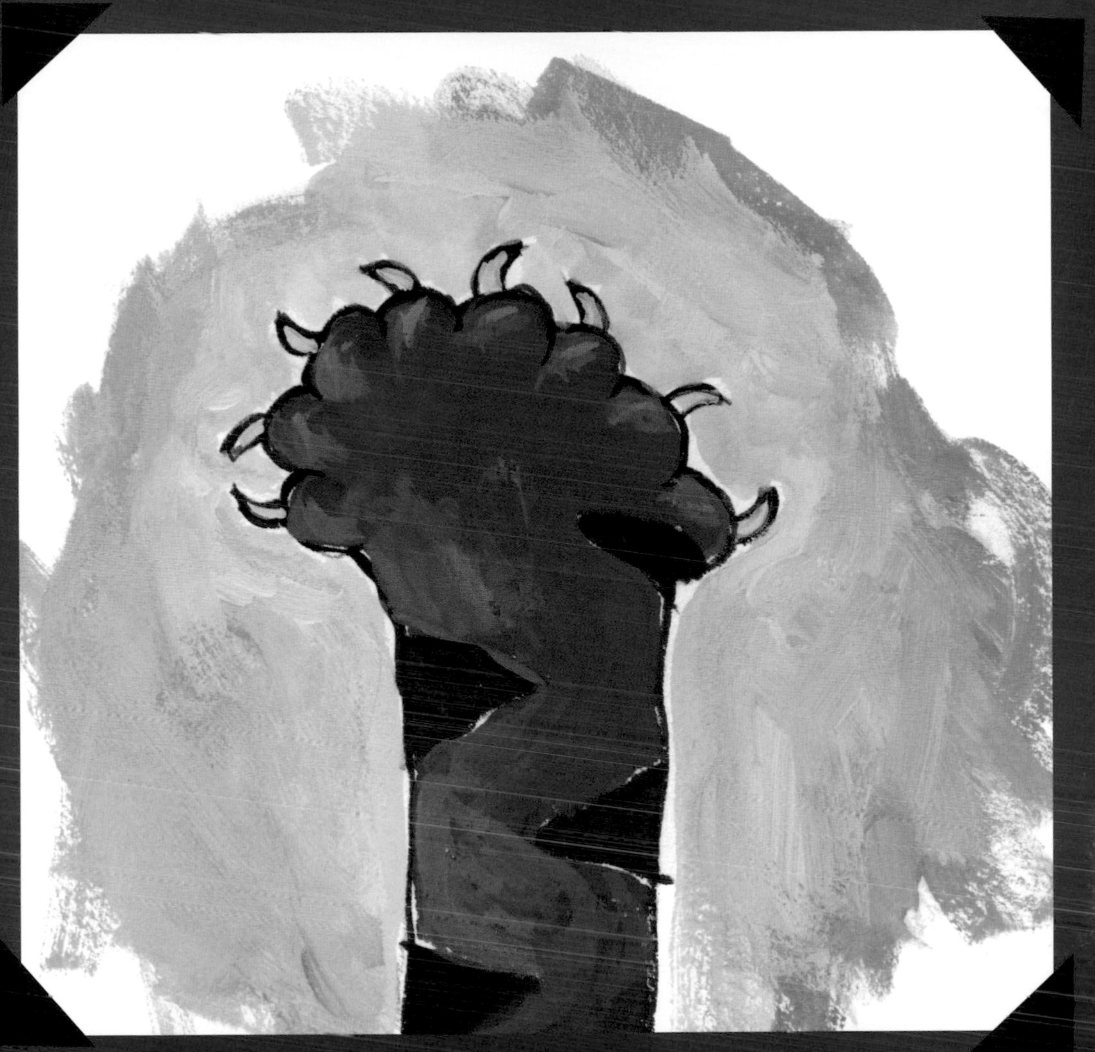

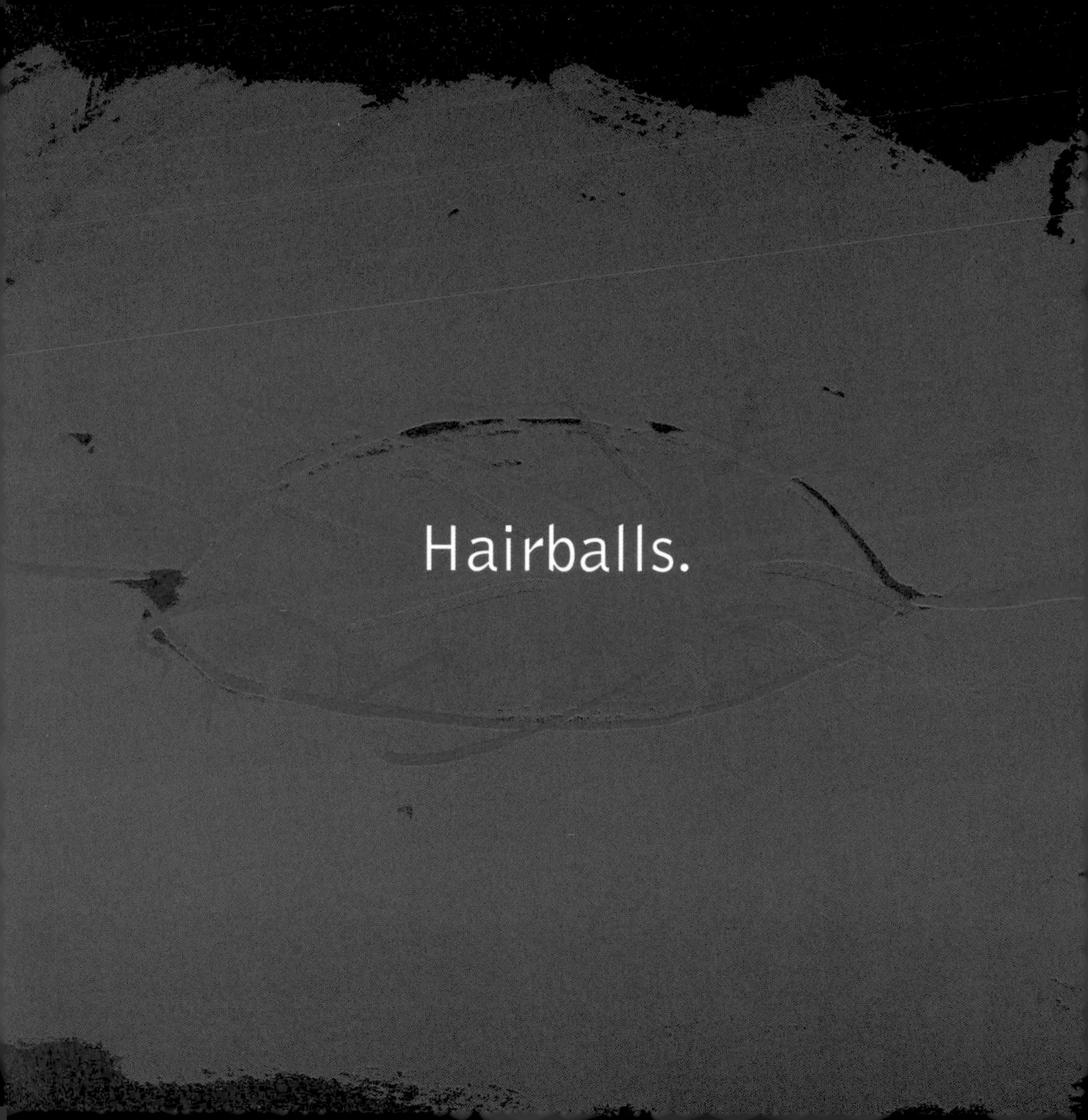
Hairballs.

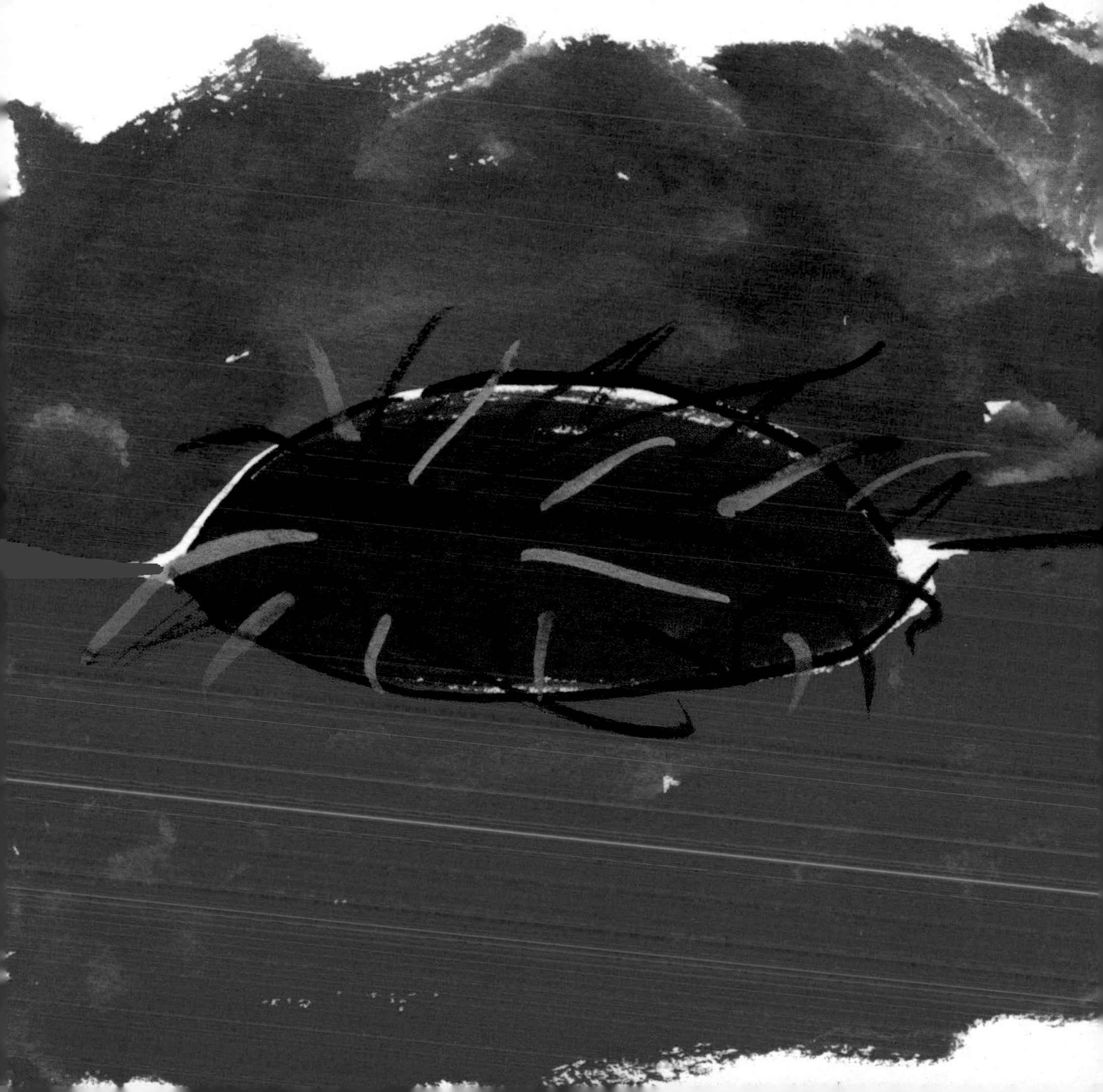

Live bugs – Ick!

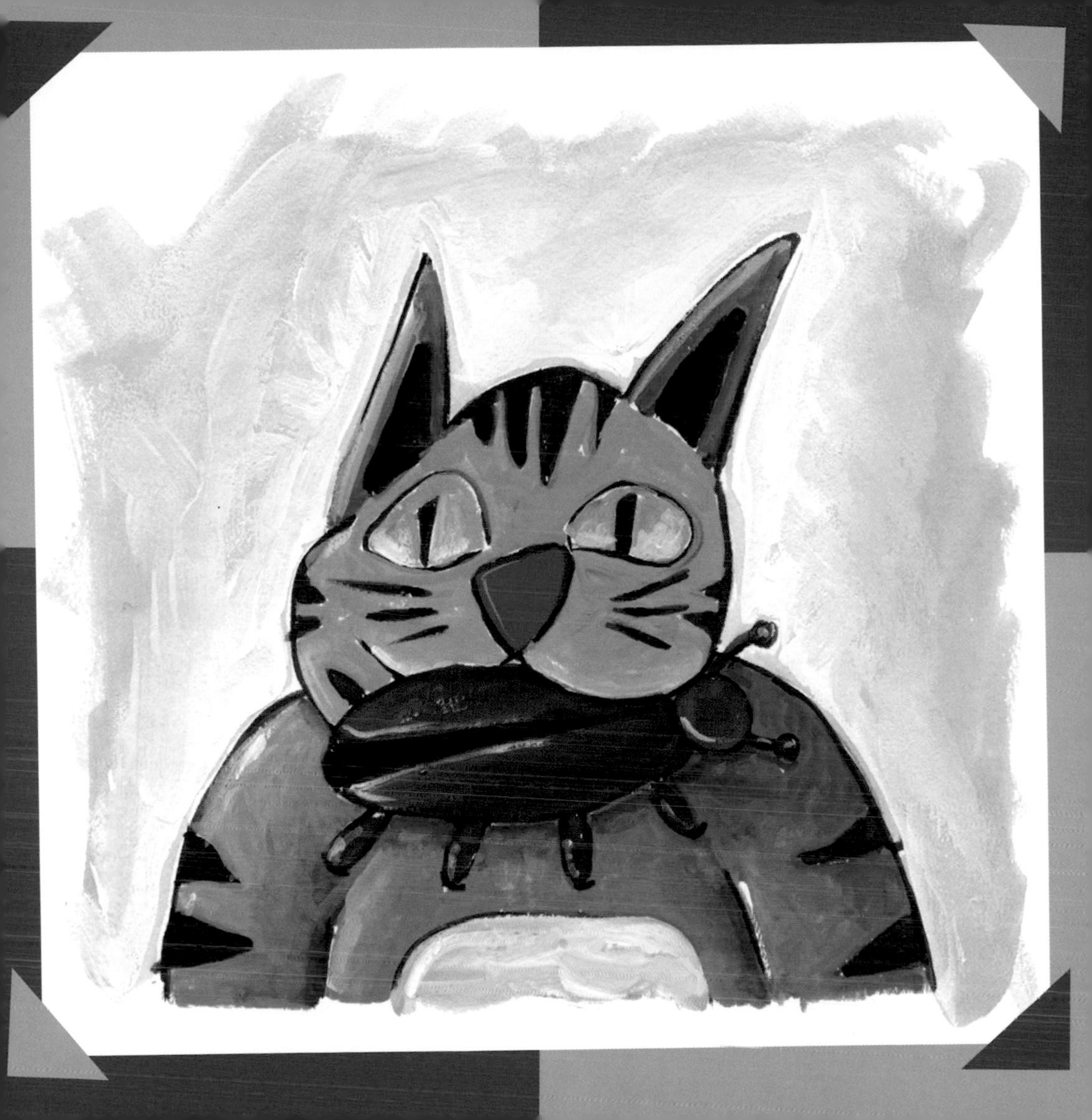

VET BILLS.

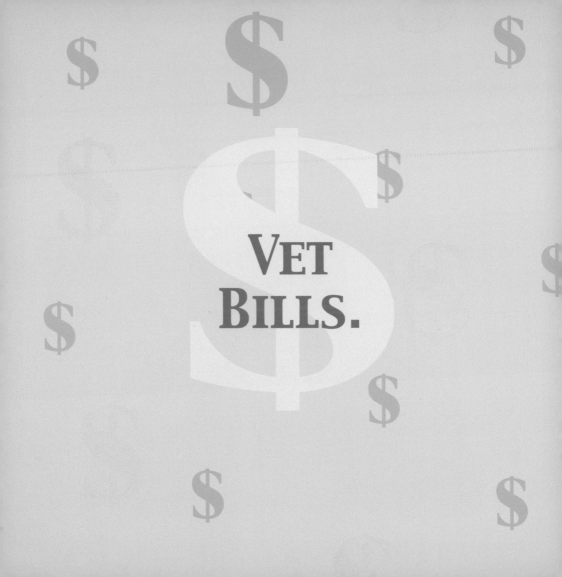

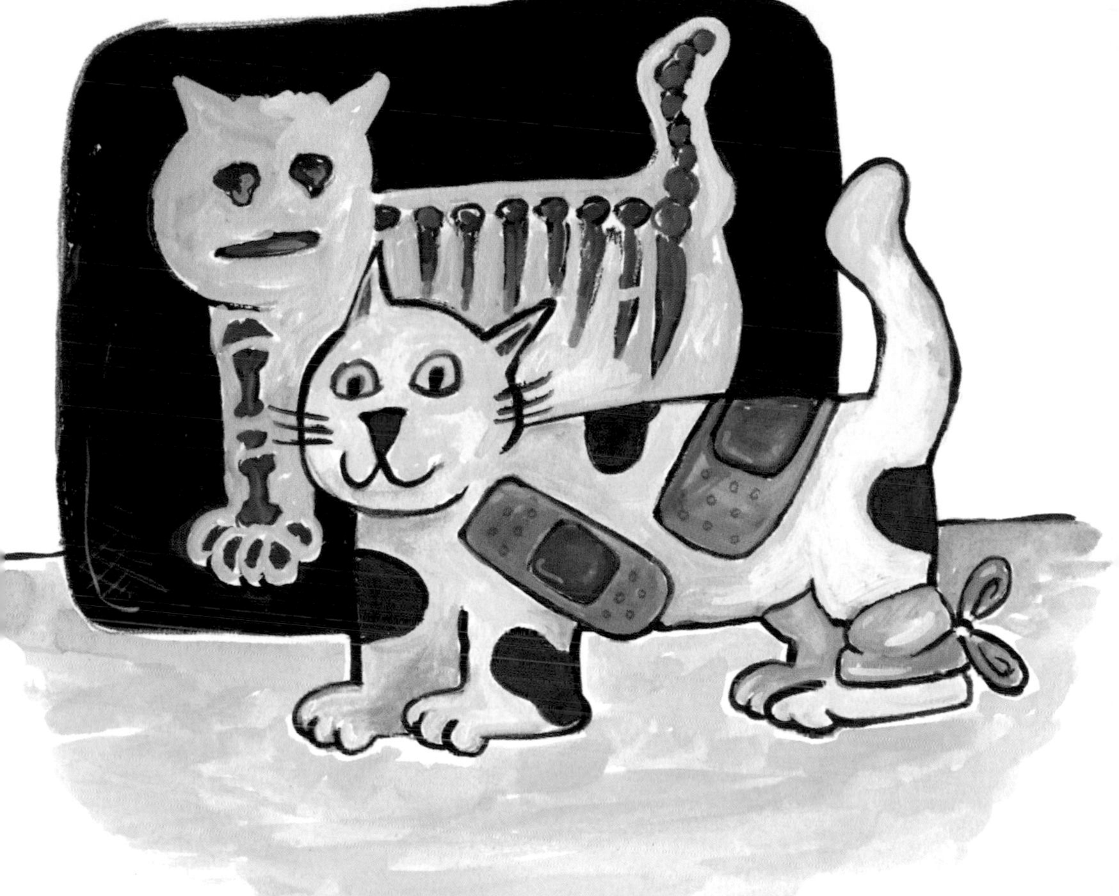

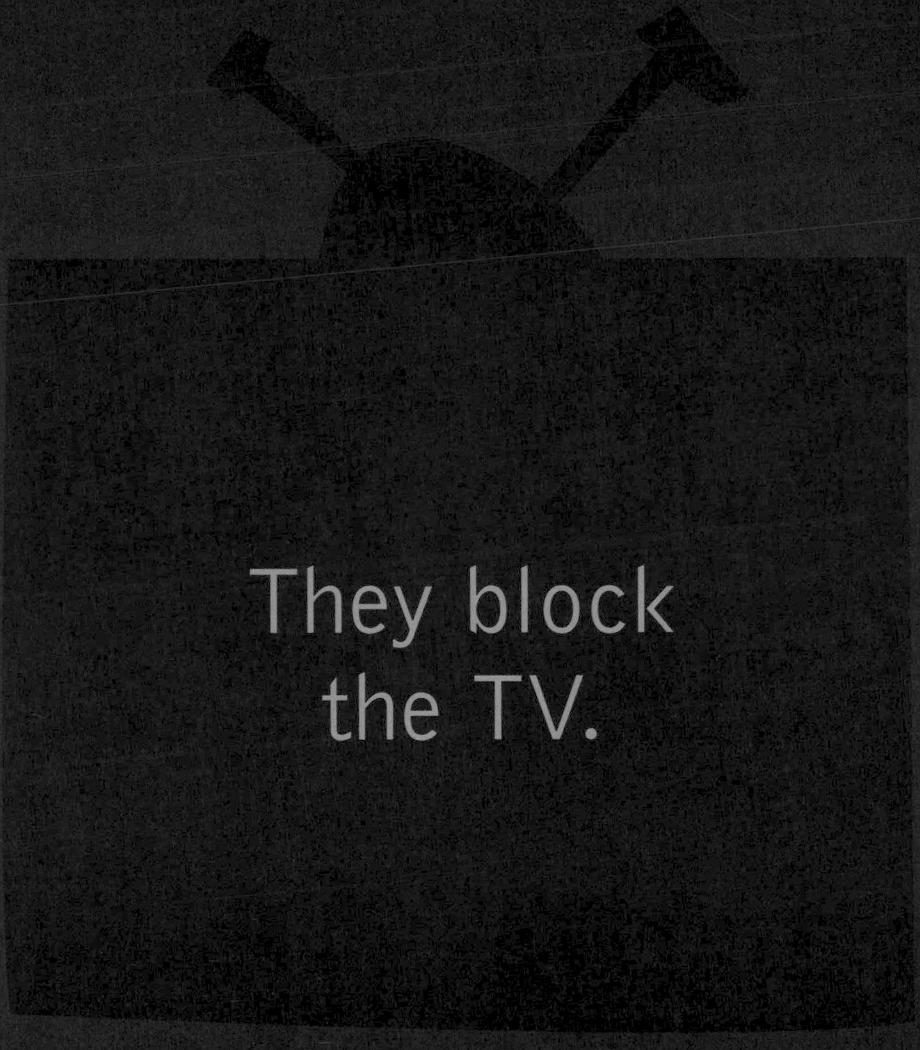

They block
the TV.

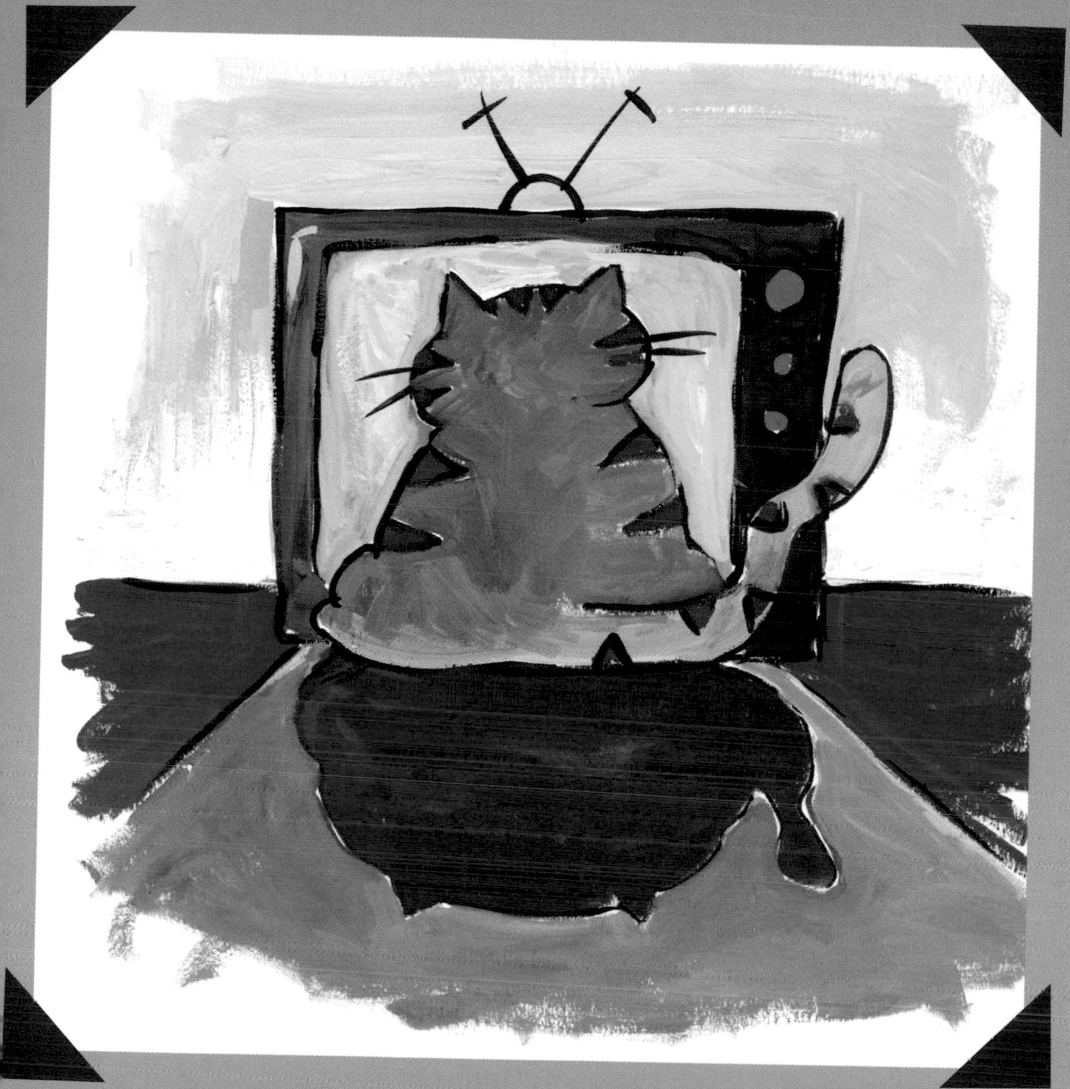

They

are

<u>so</u>

analog.

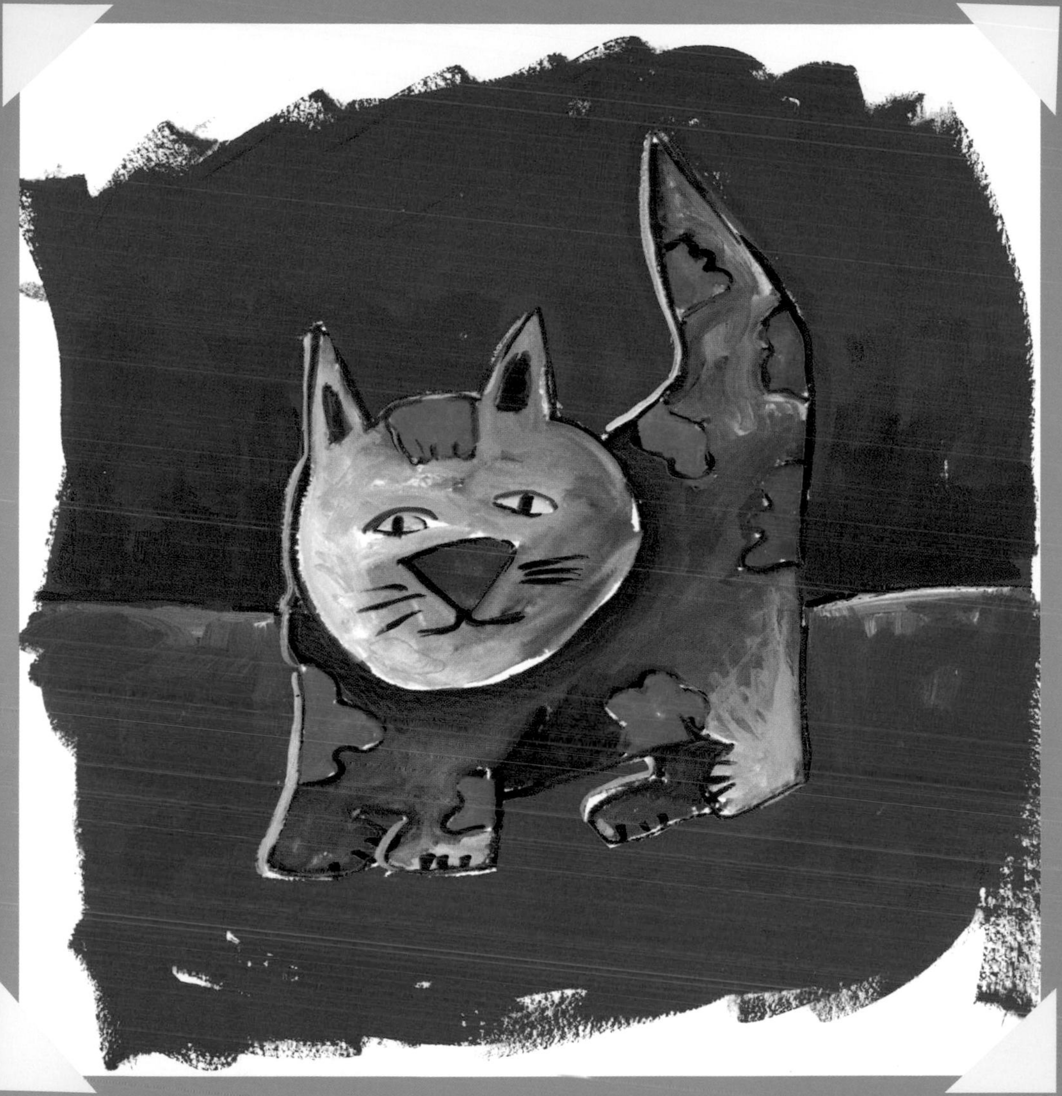

They can see at night.

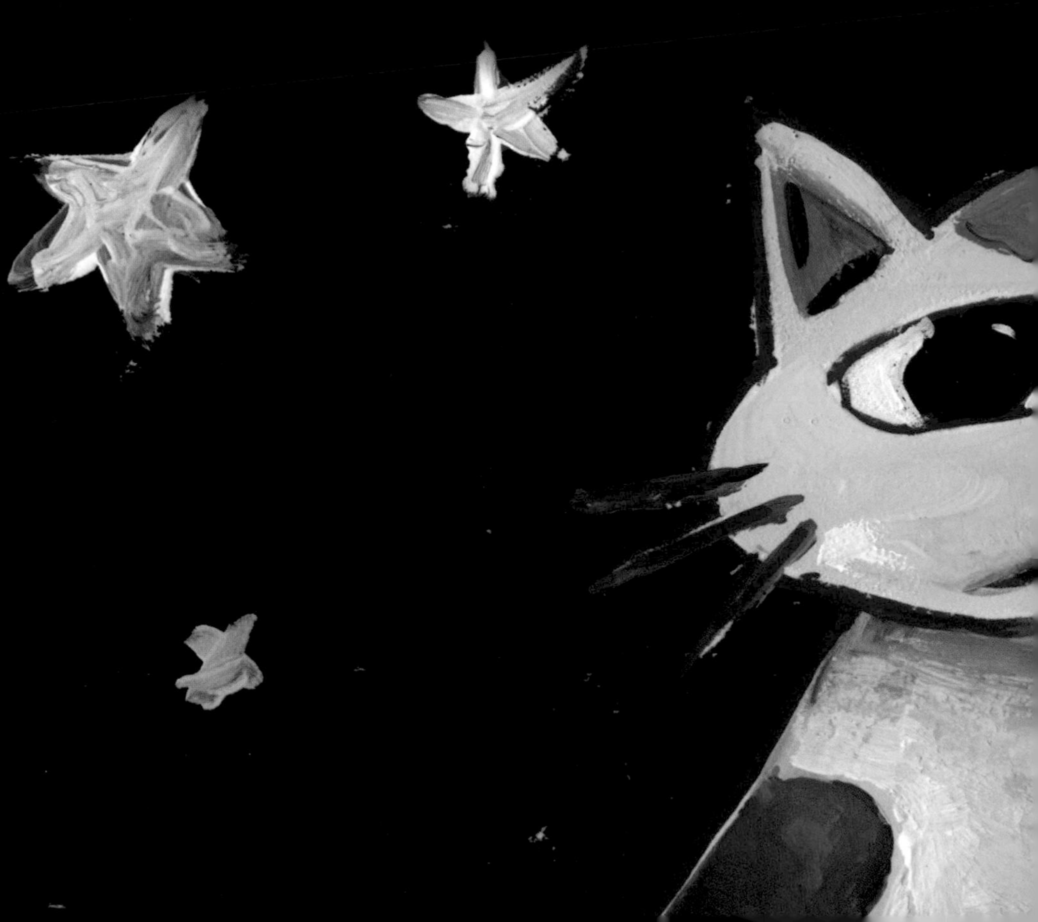

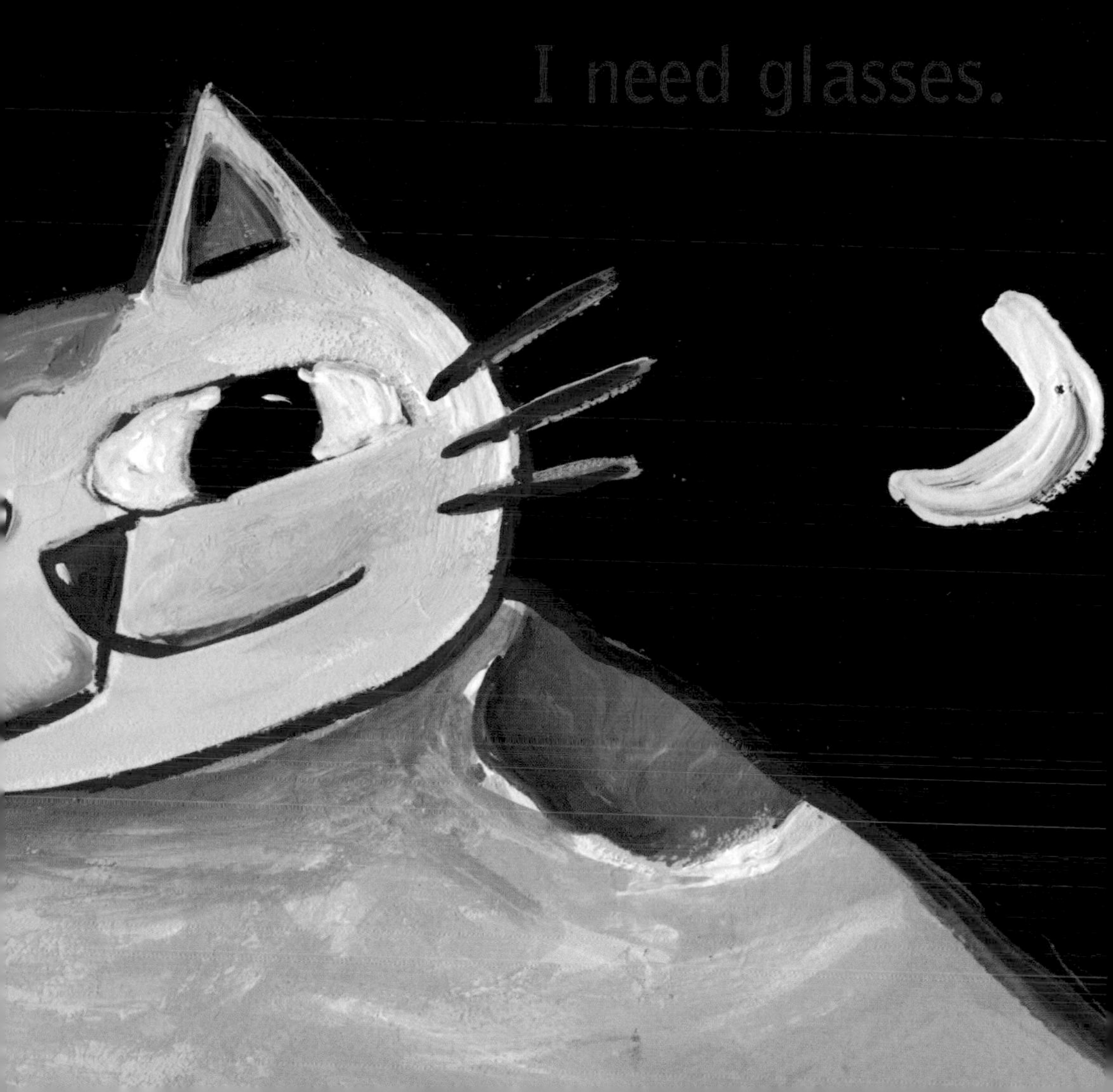
I need glasses.

They eat
each other's puke.

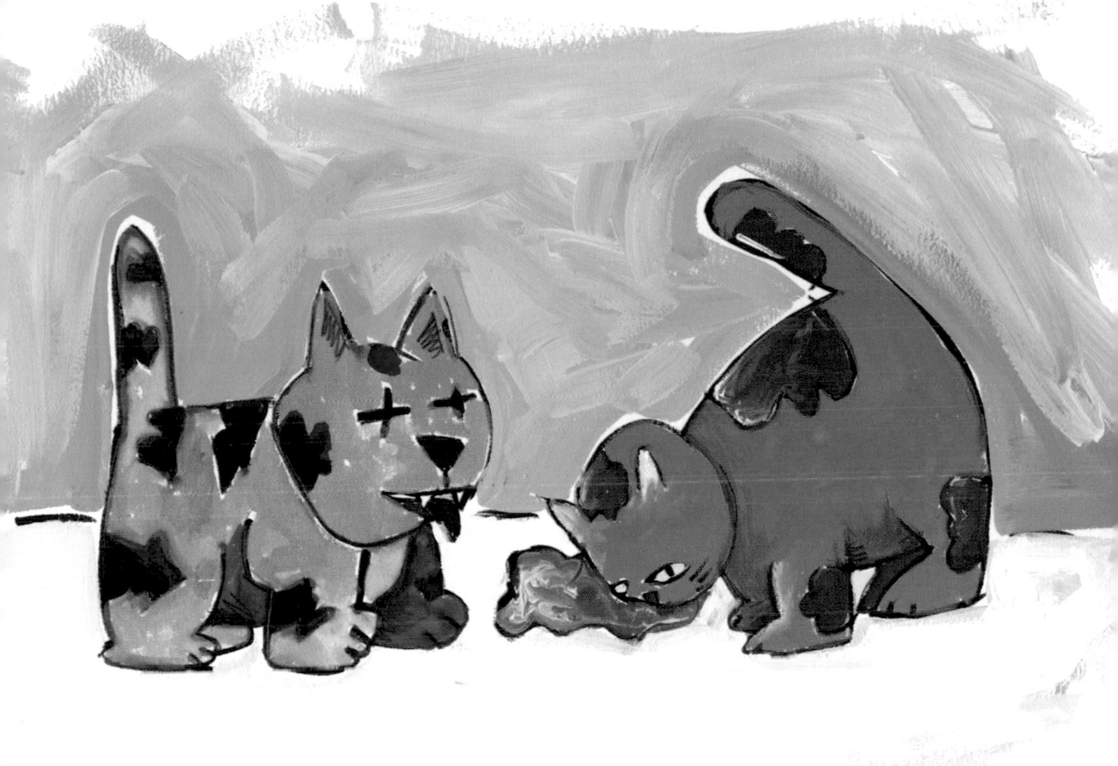

They change
the channel.

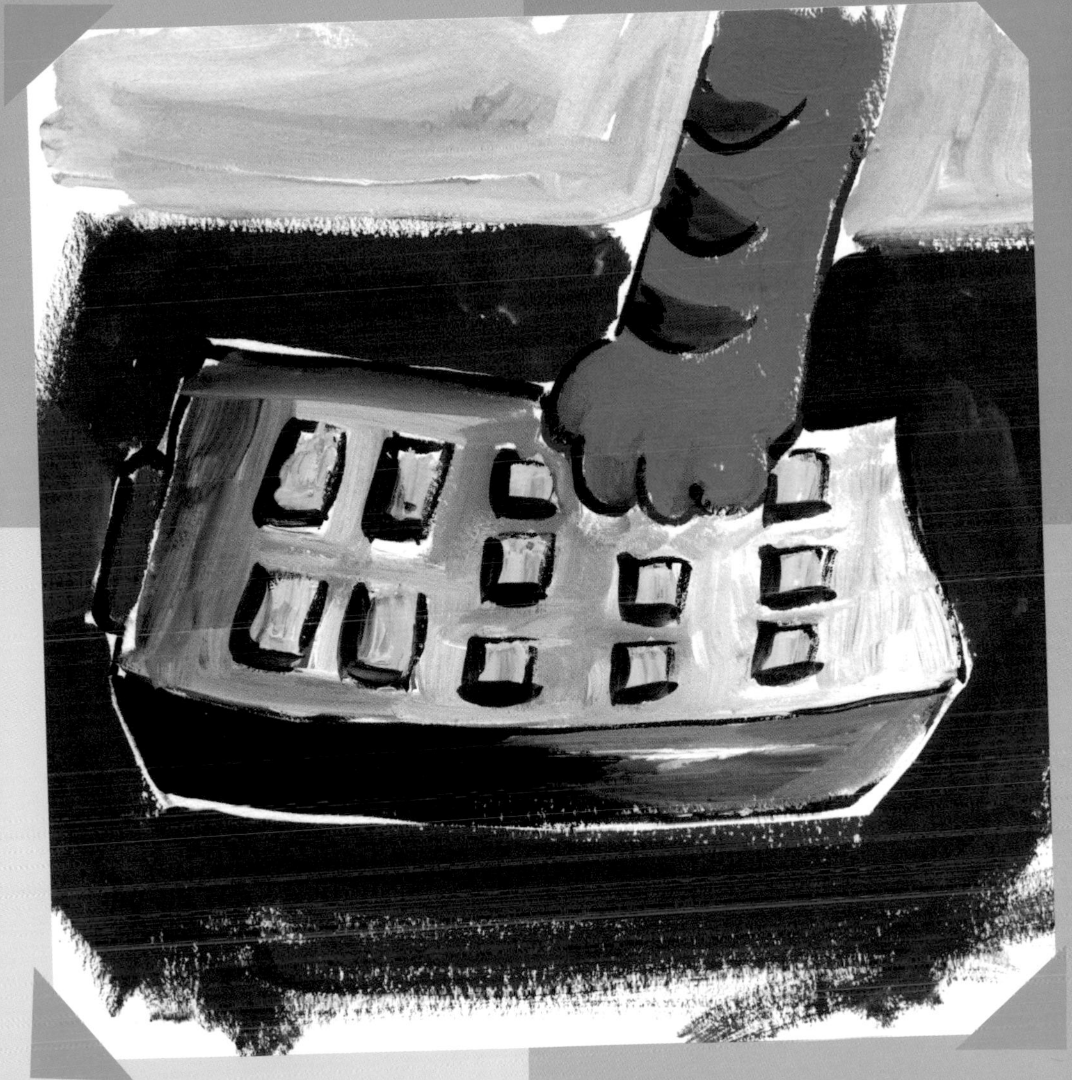

They stare at me.

Why?

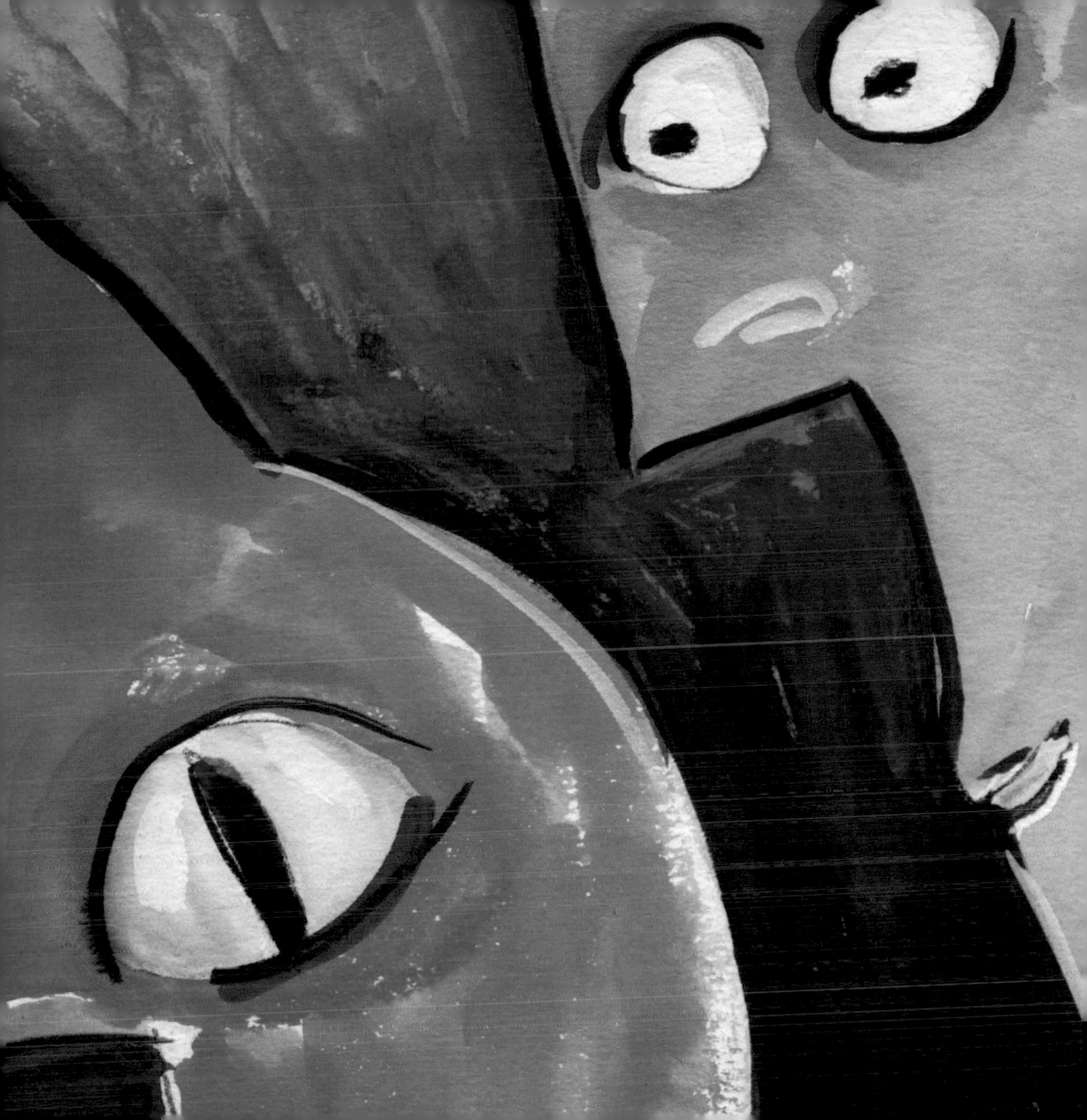

They sleep
on my head.

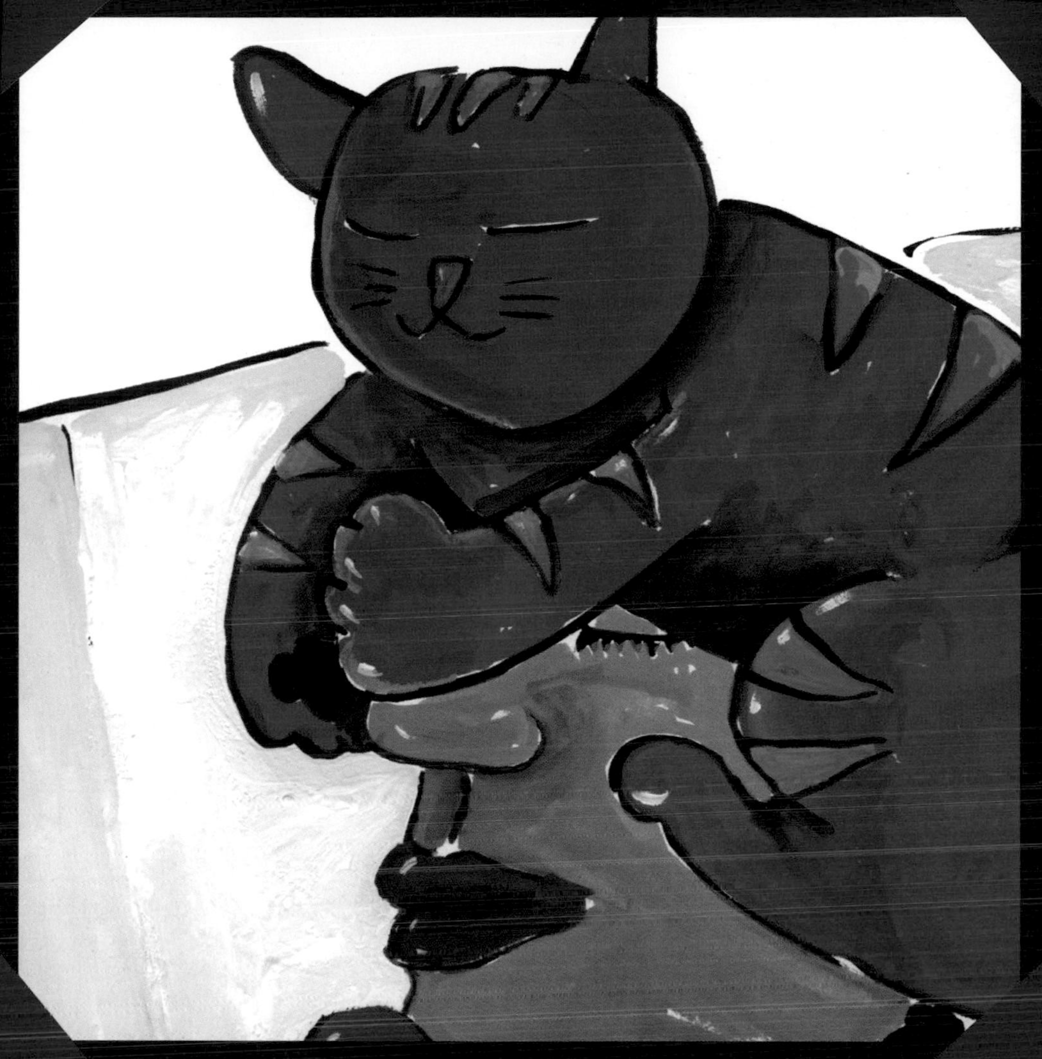

They unroll the
last roll
of toilet paper.

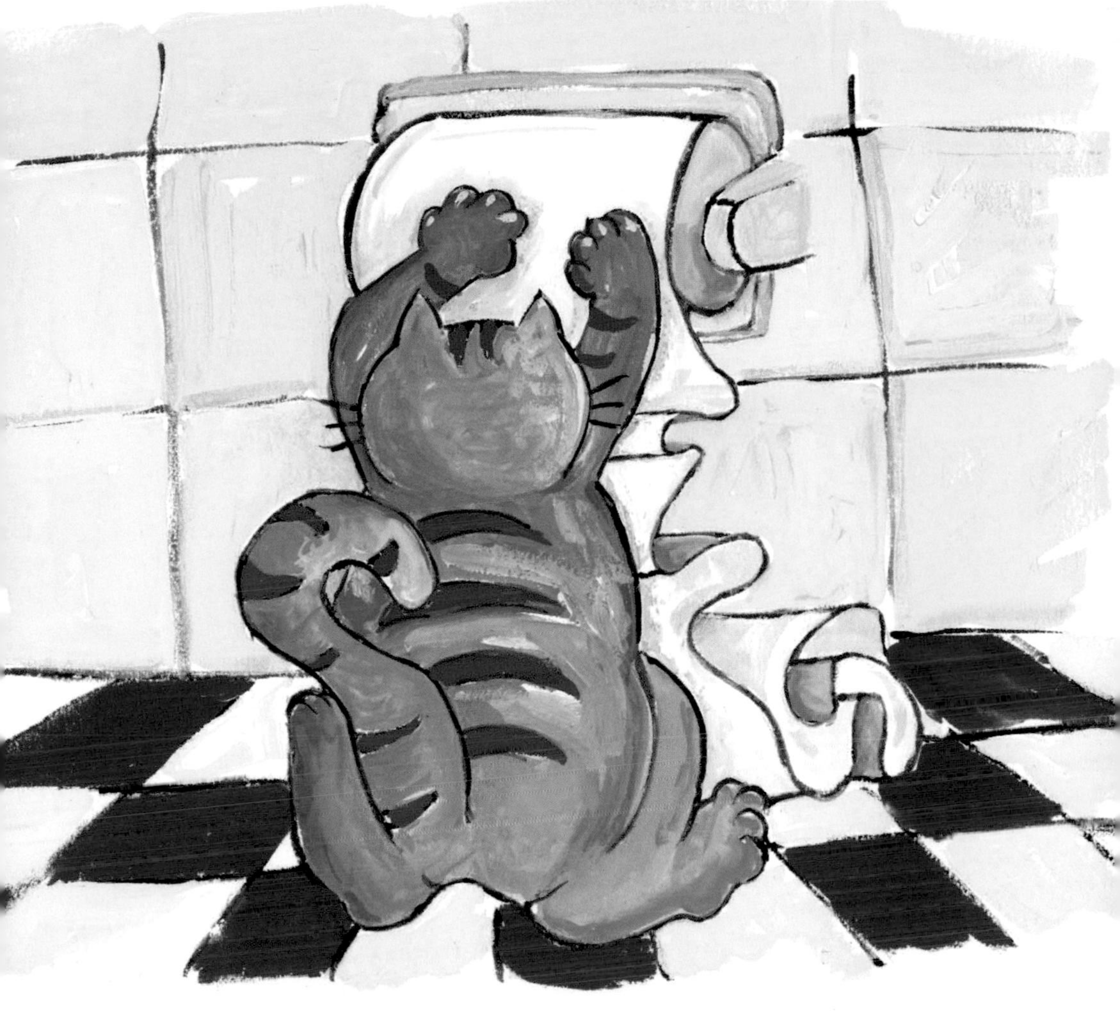

They
eat
my
plants.

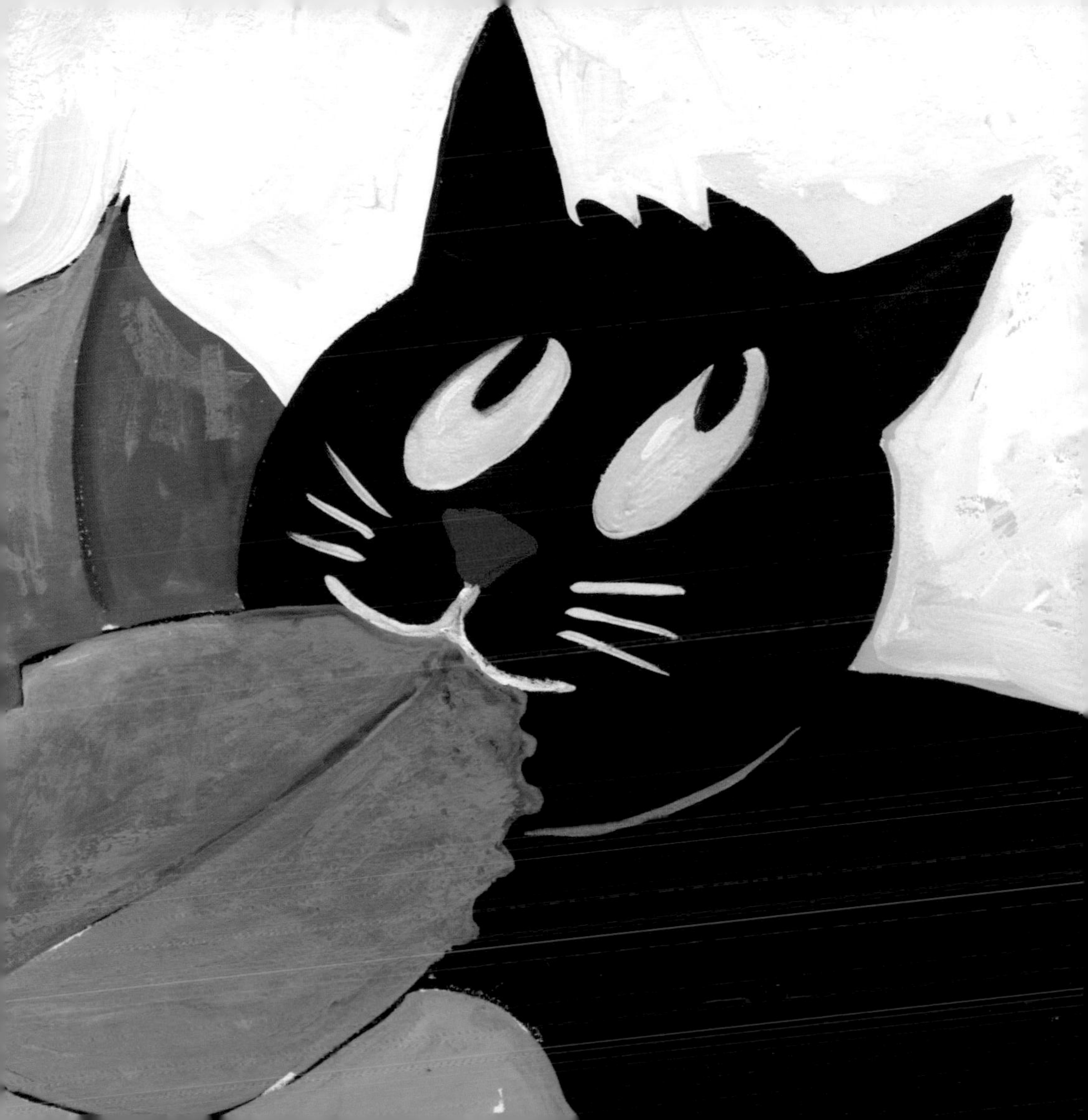

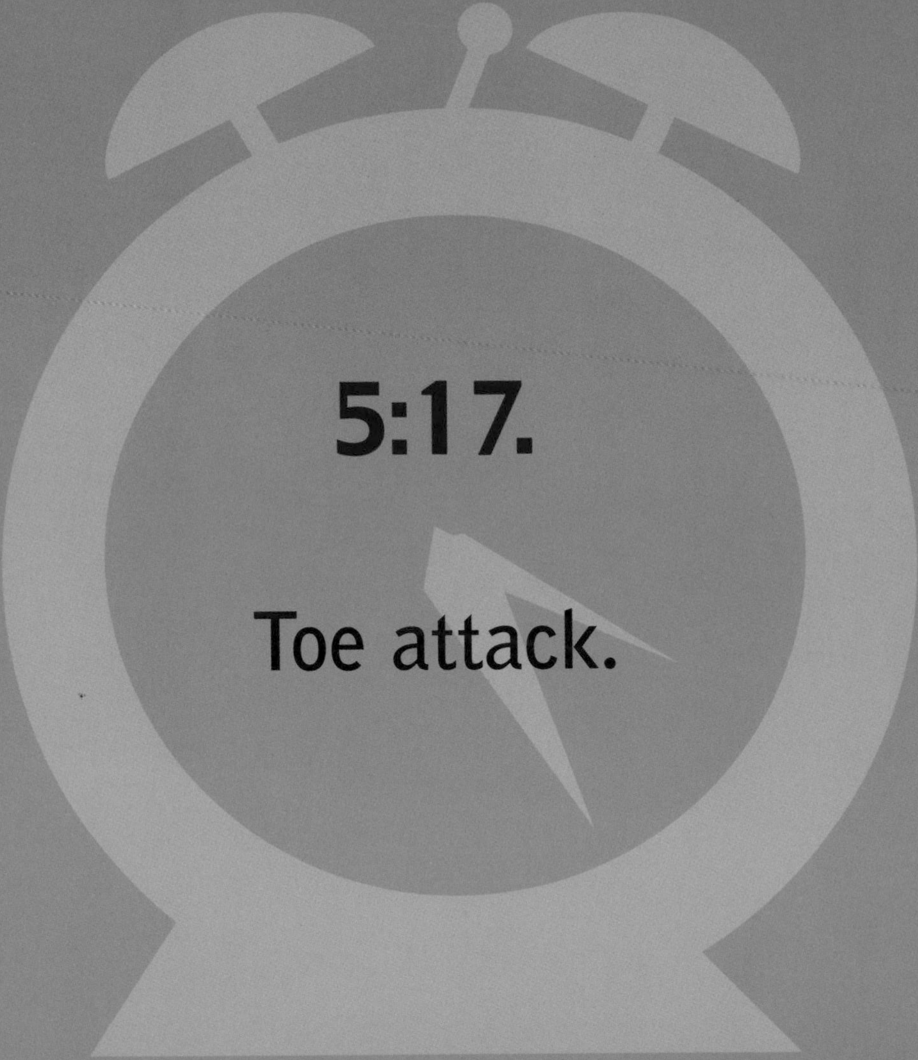
5:17.
Toe attack.

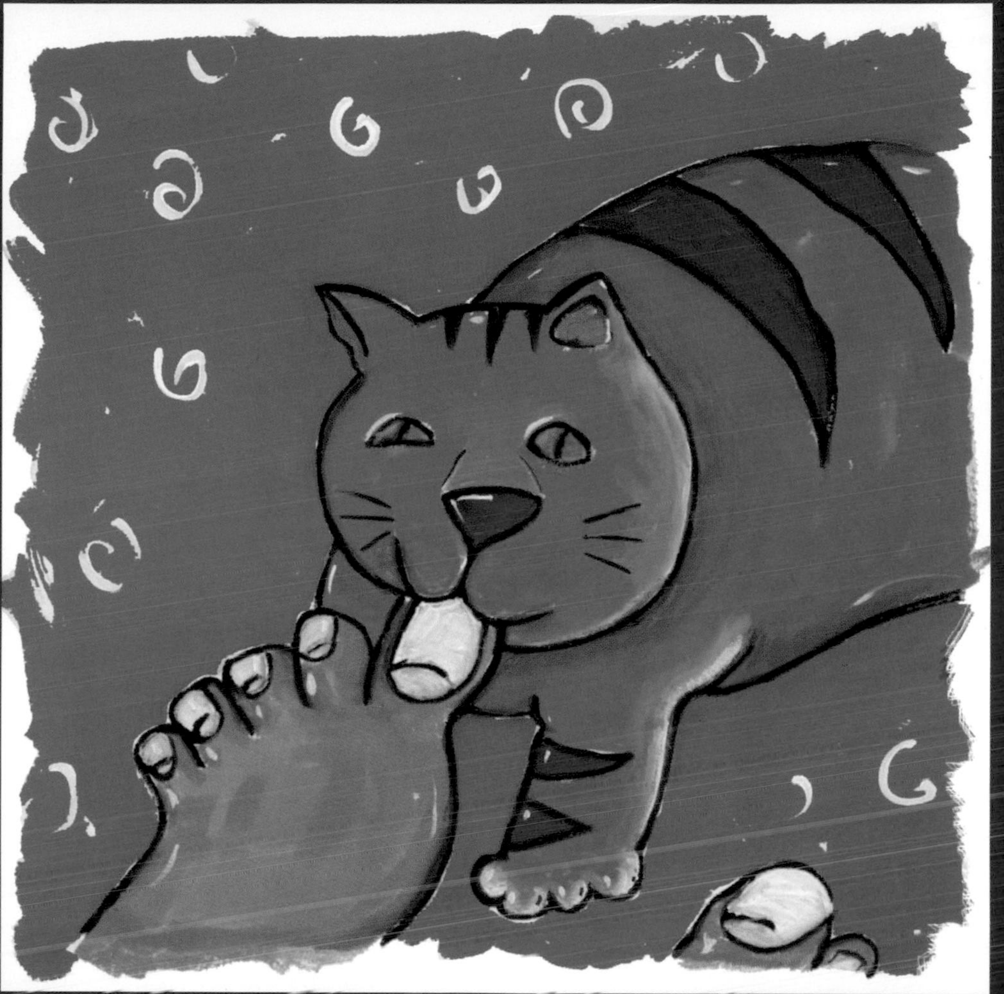

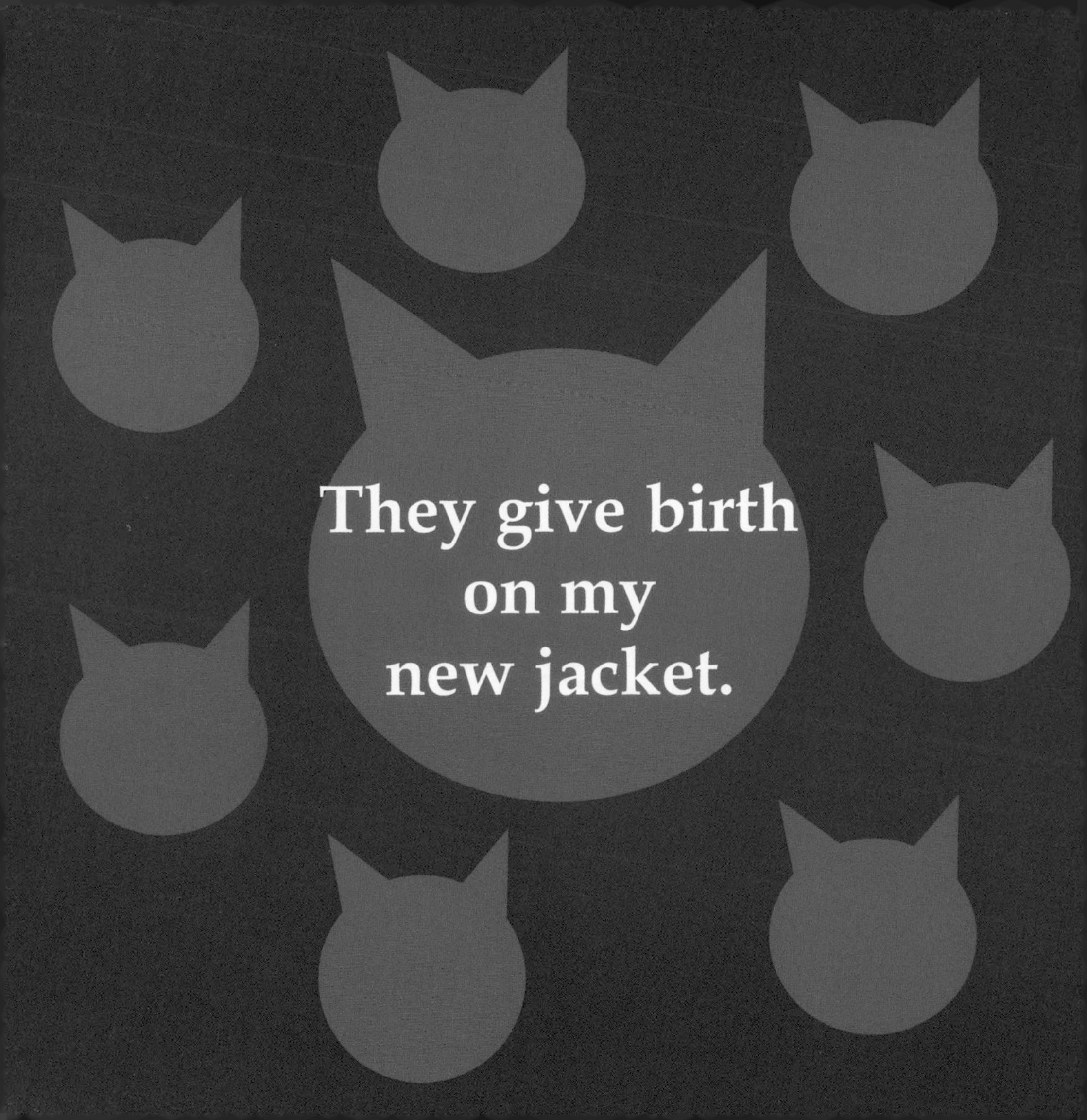
They give birth
on my
new jacket.

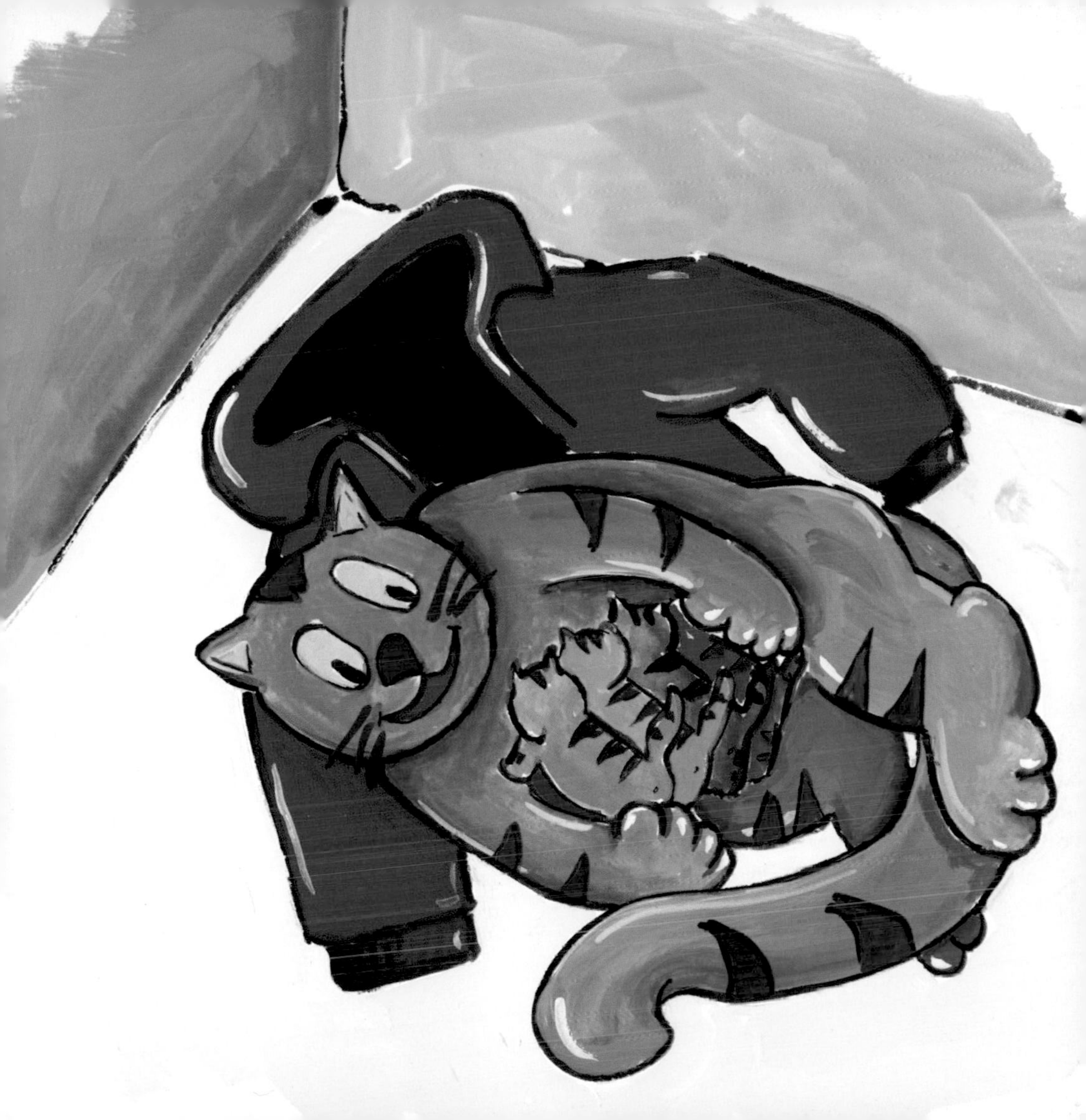

Read my mind:

TURKEY

TURKEY

TURKEY

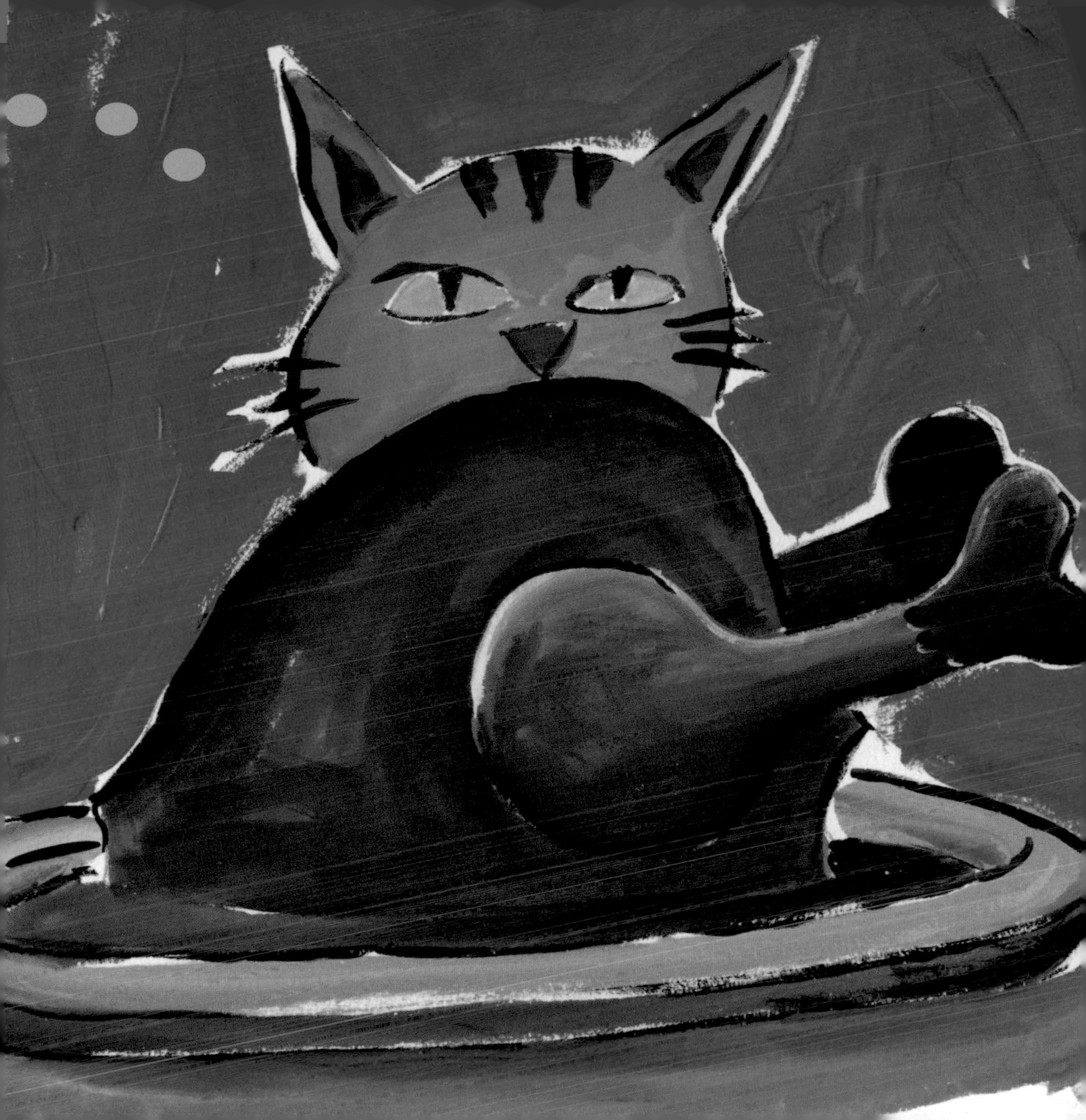

Does this look like a refreshing mountain spring

?

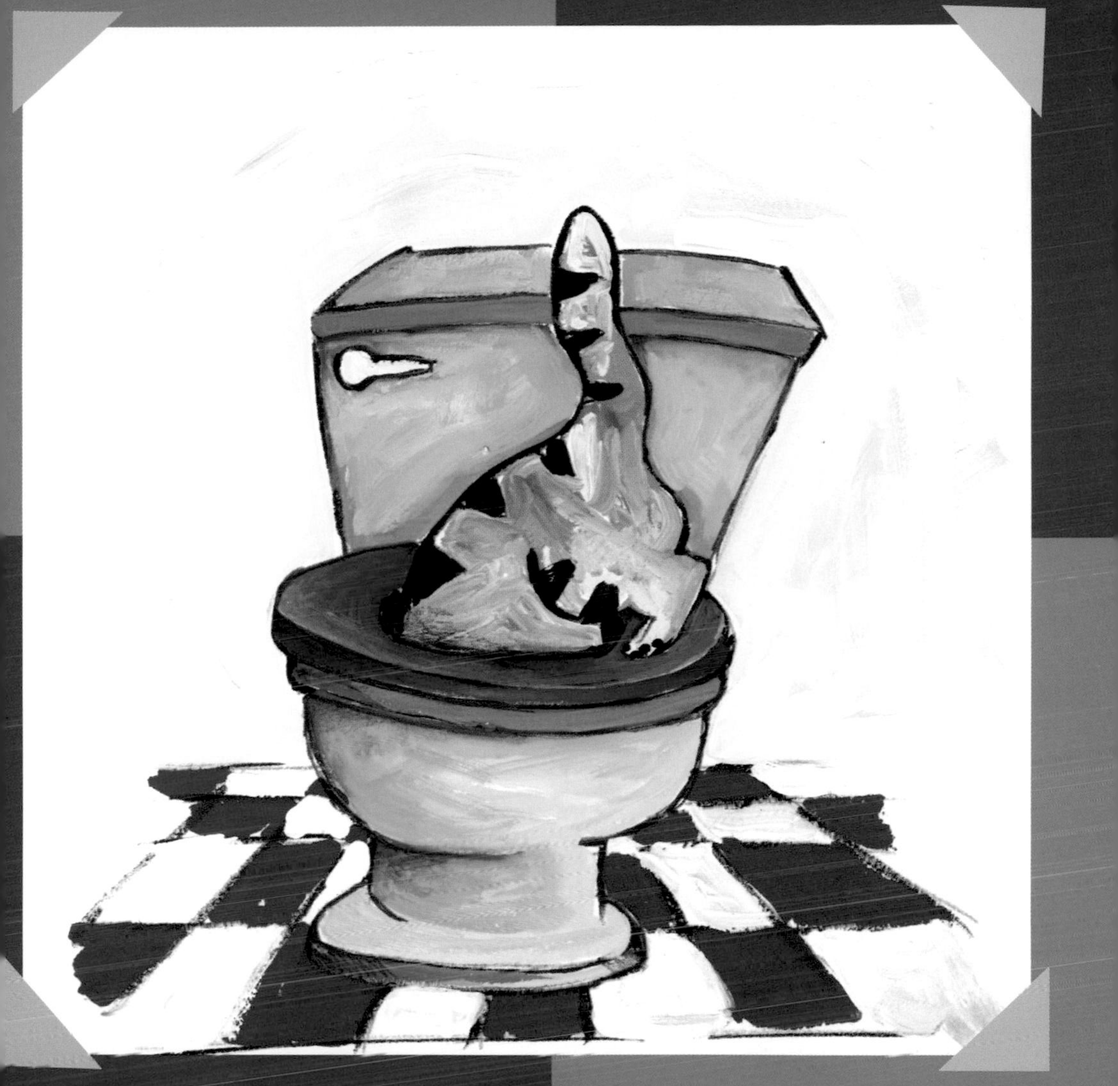

My
watch
IS
NOT
a
hockey
puck.

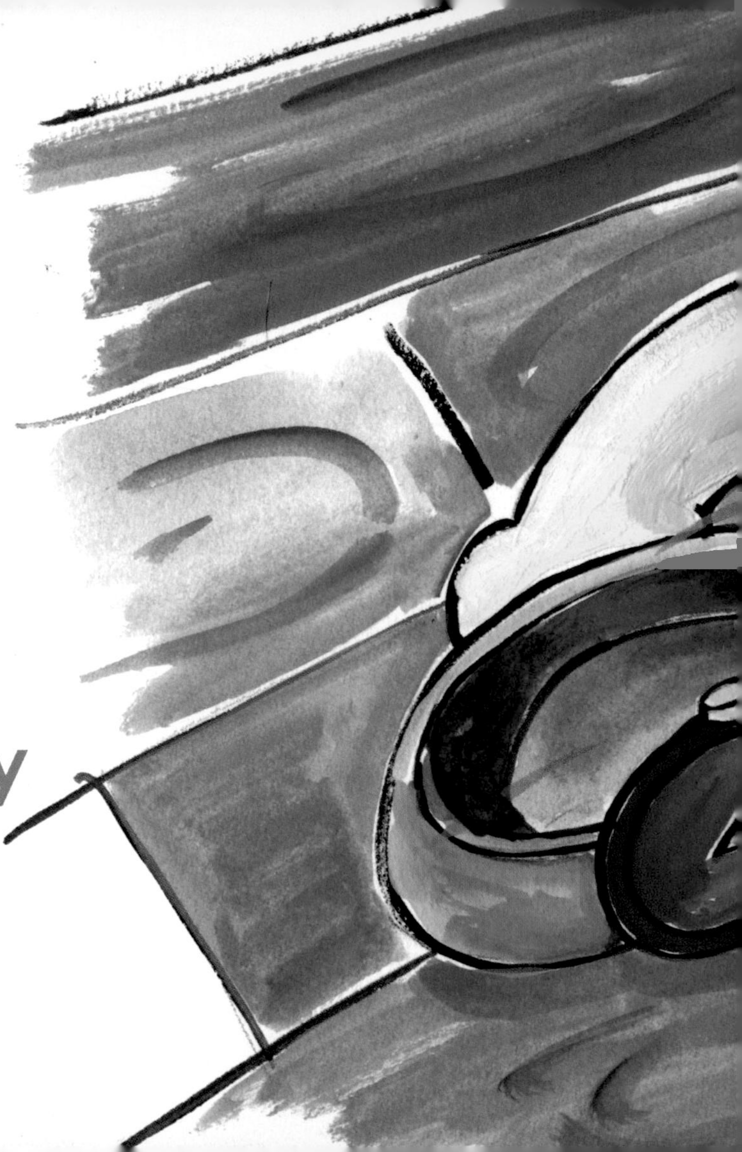

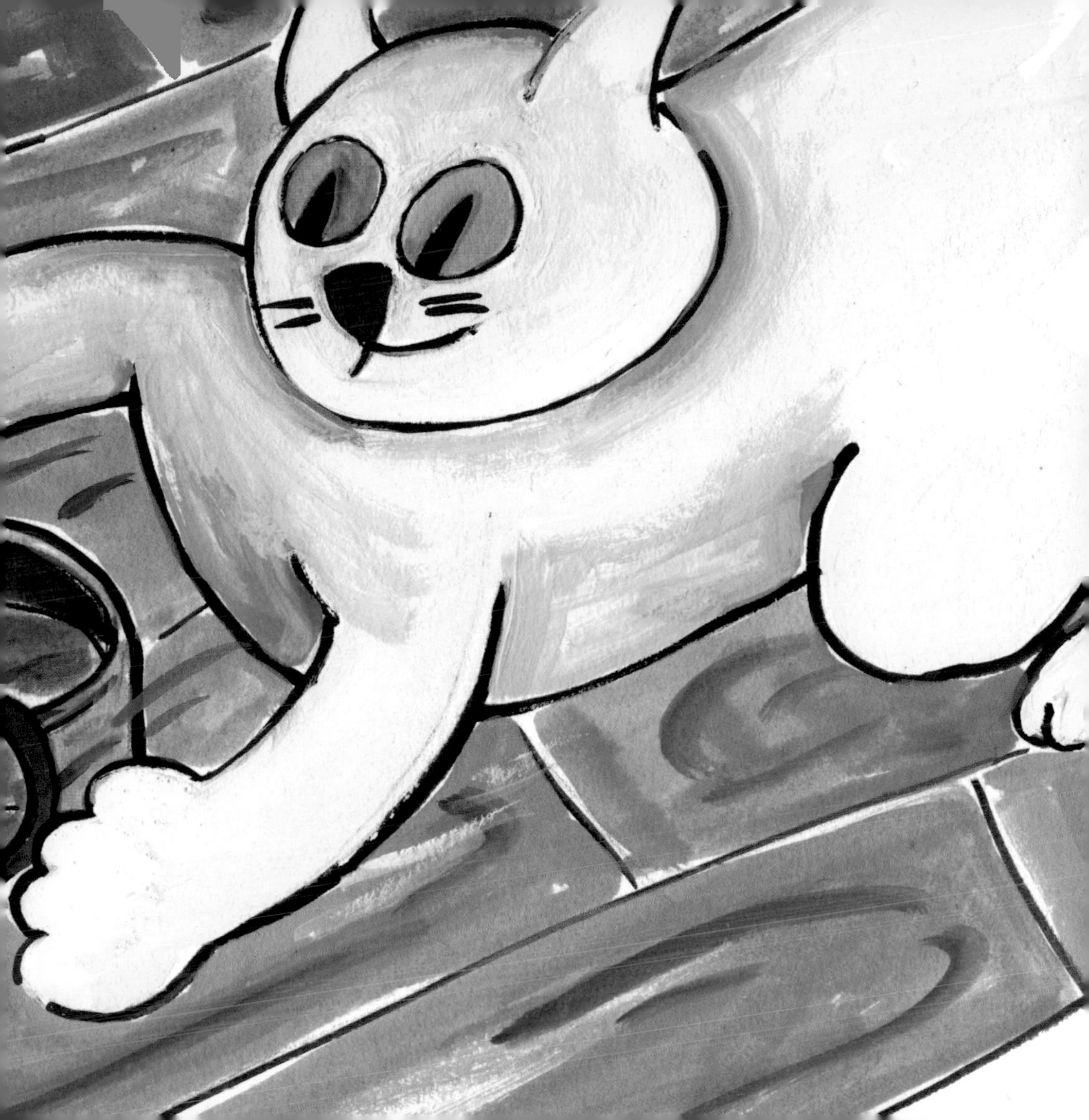

Paw prints

on my

clean car.

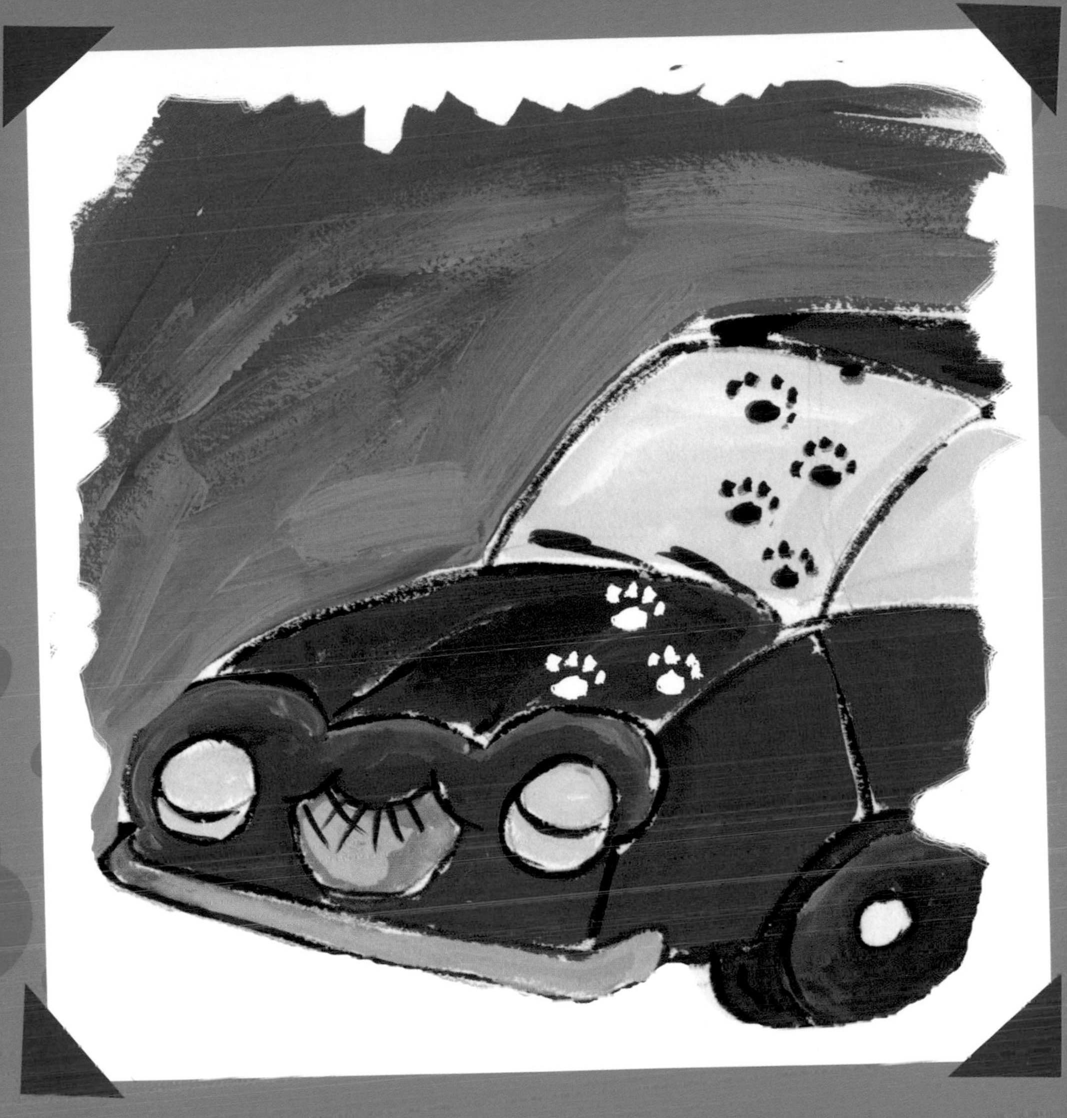

They eat

Butterflies.

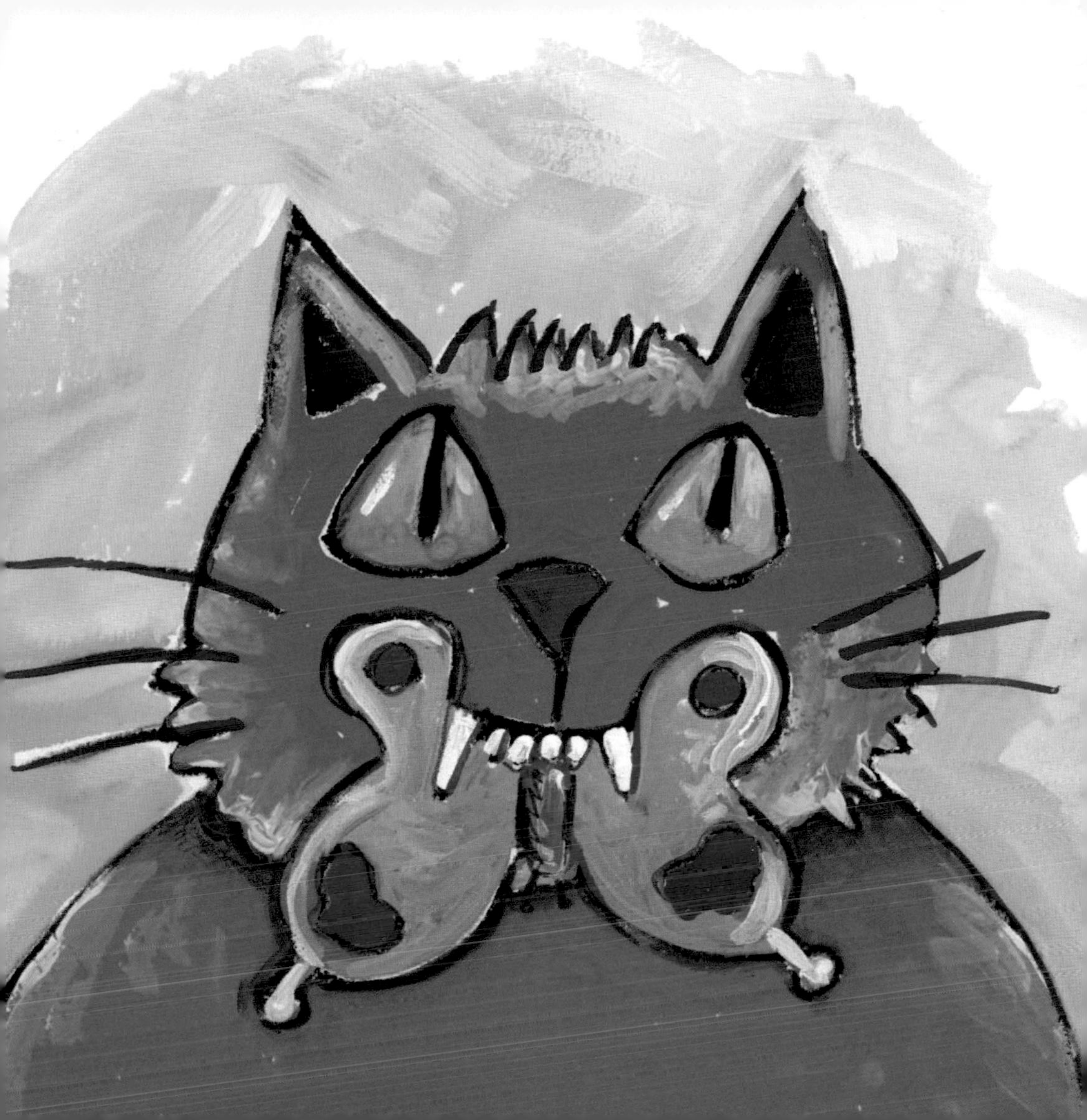

THEY HAVE

NO

TABLE MANNERS.

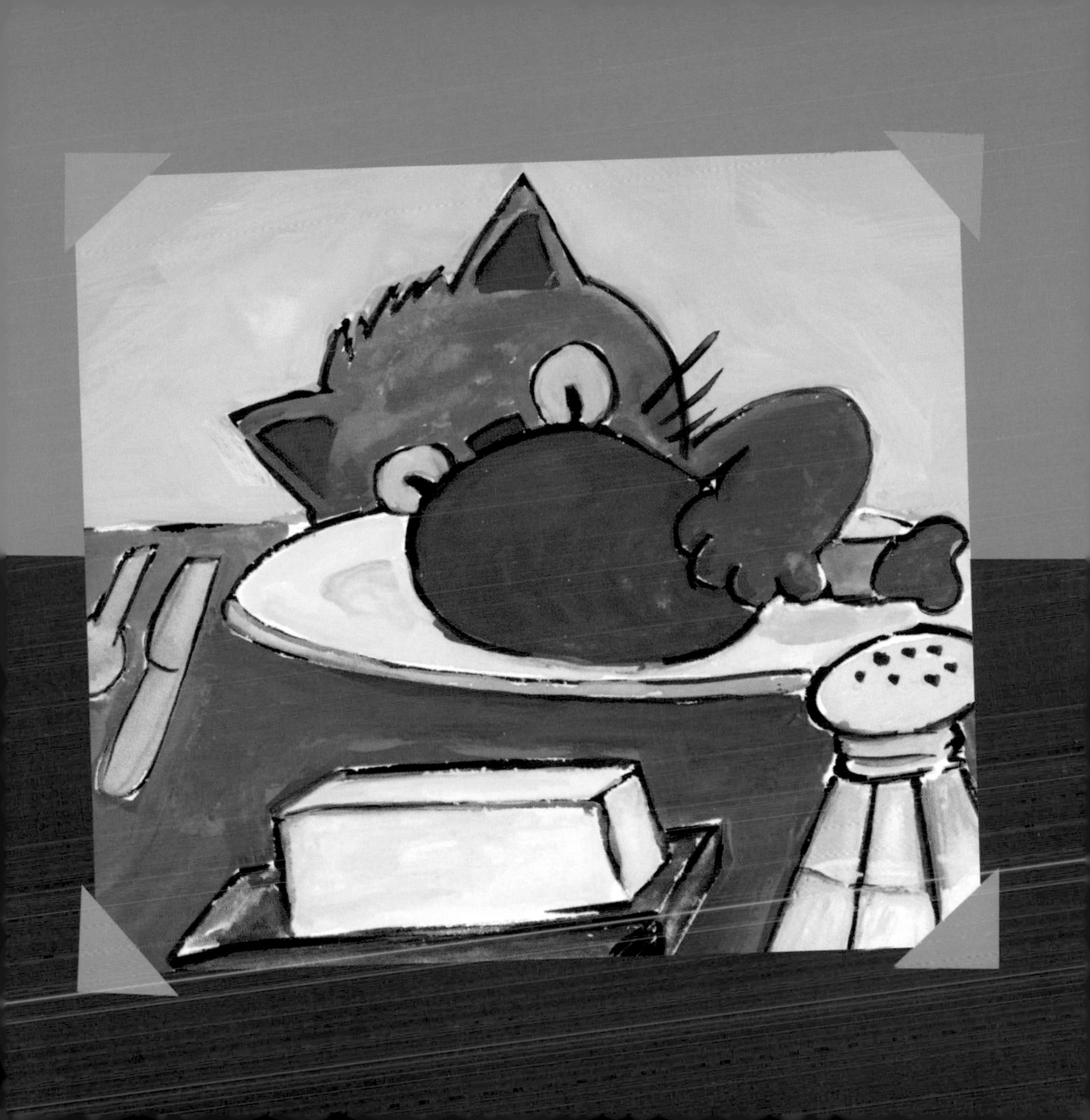

They ignore me
if I call them.

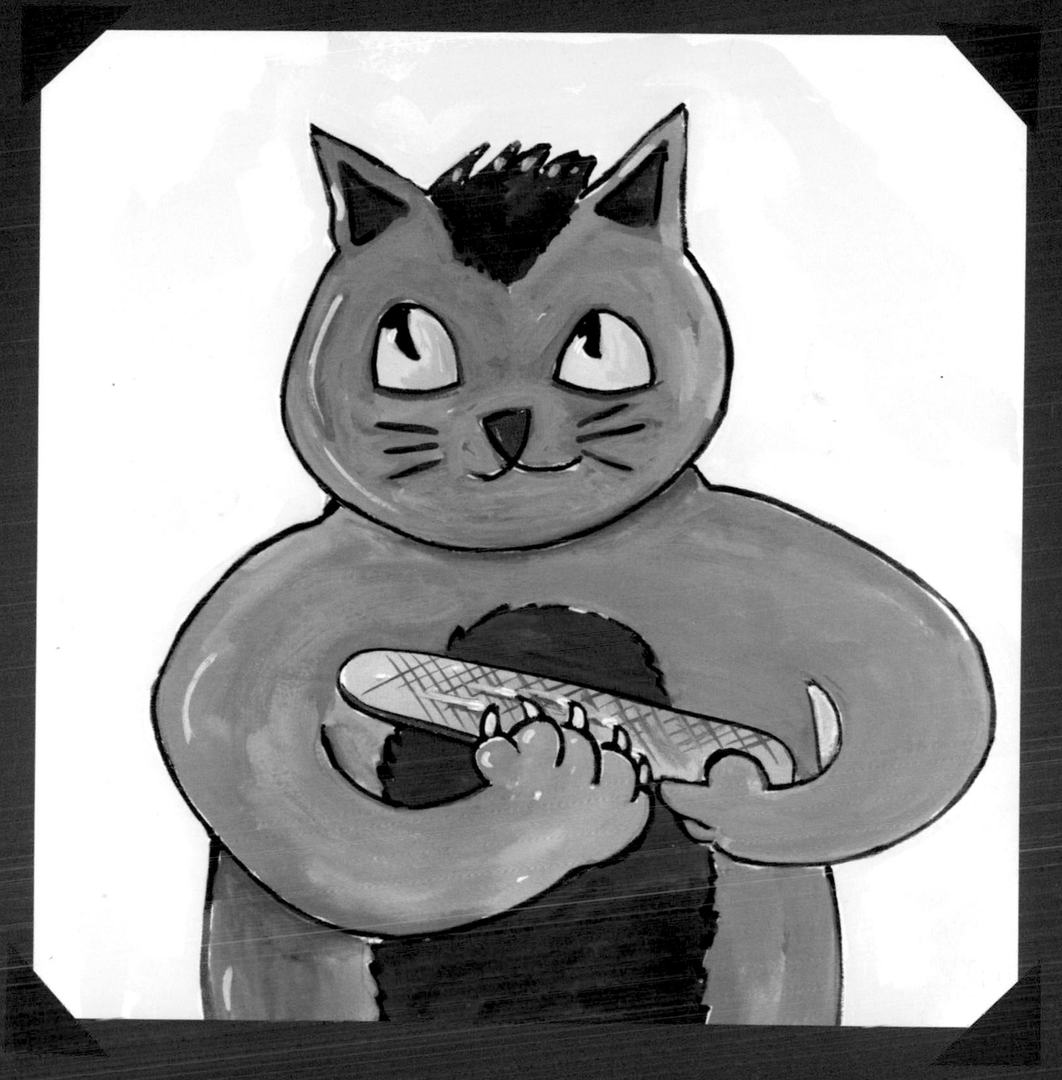

If I open
any can
they come a-runnin'.

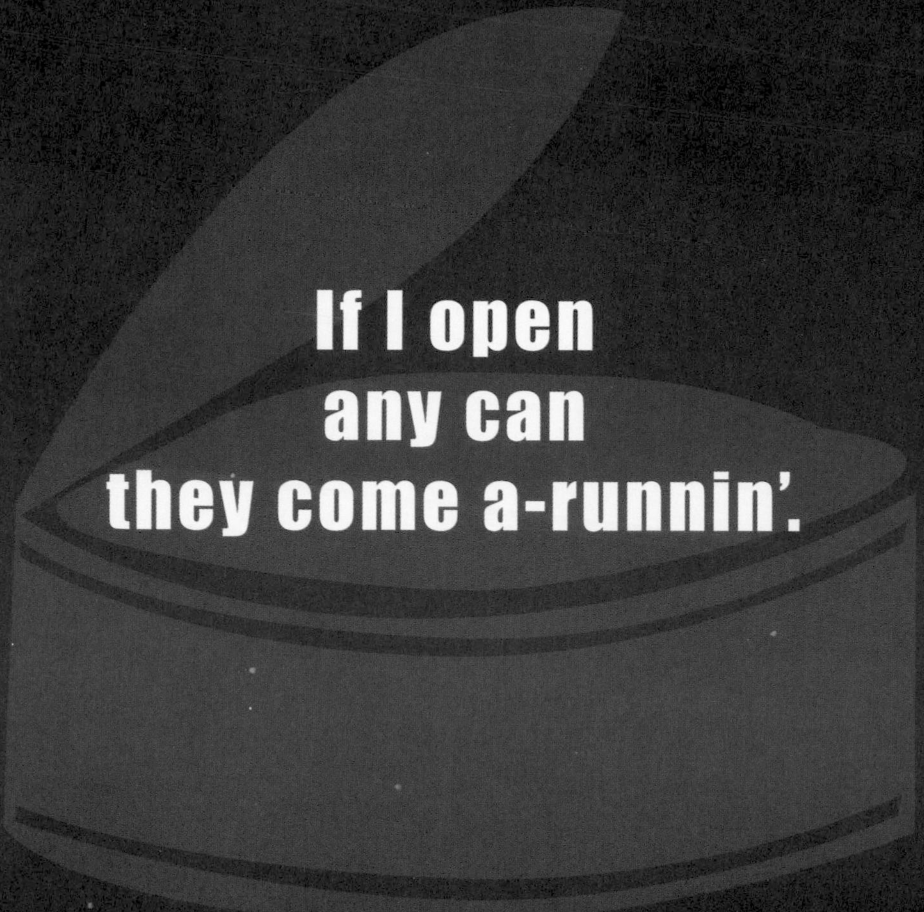

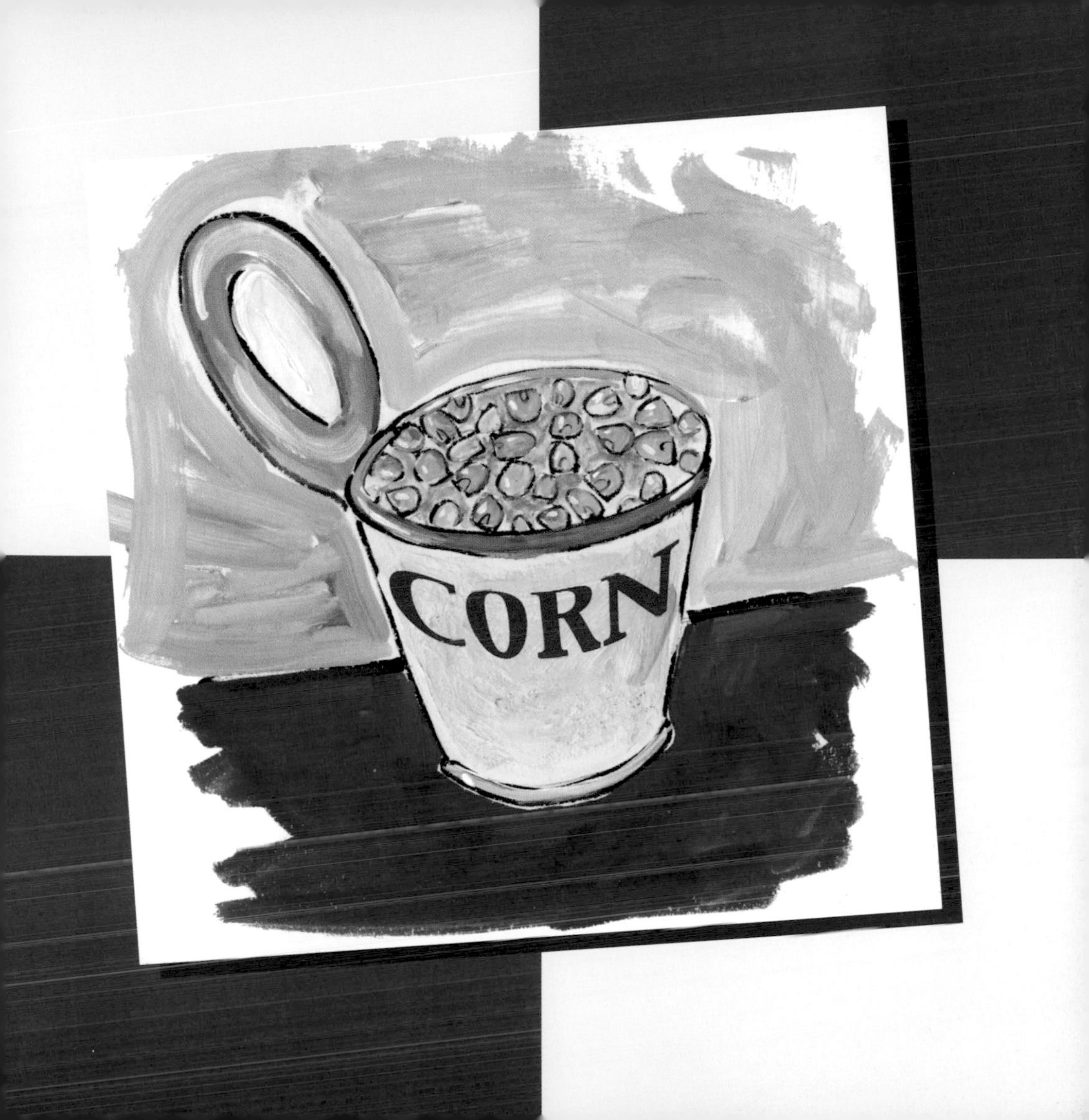
CORN

When guests visit
they hide
under the bed.

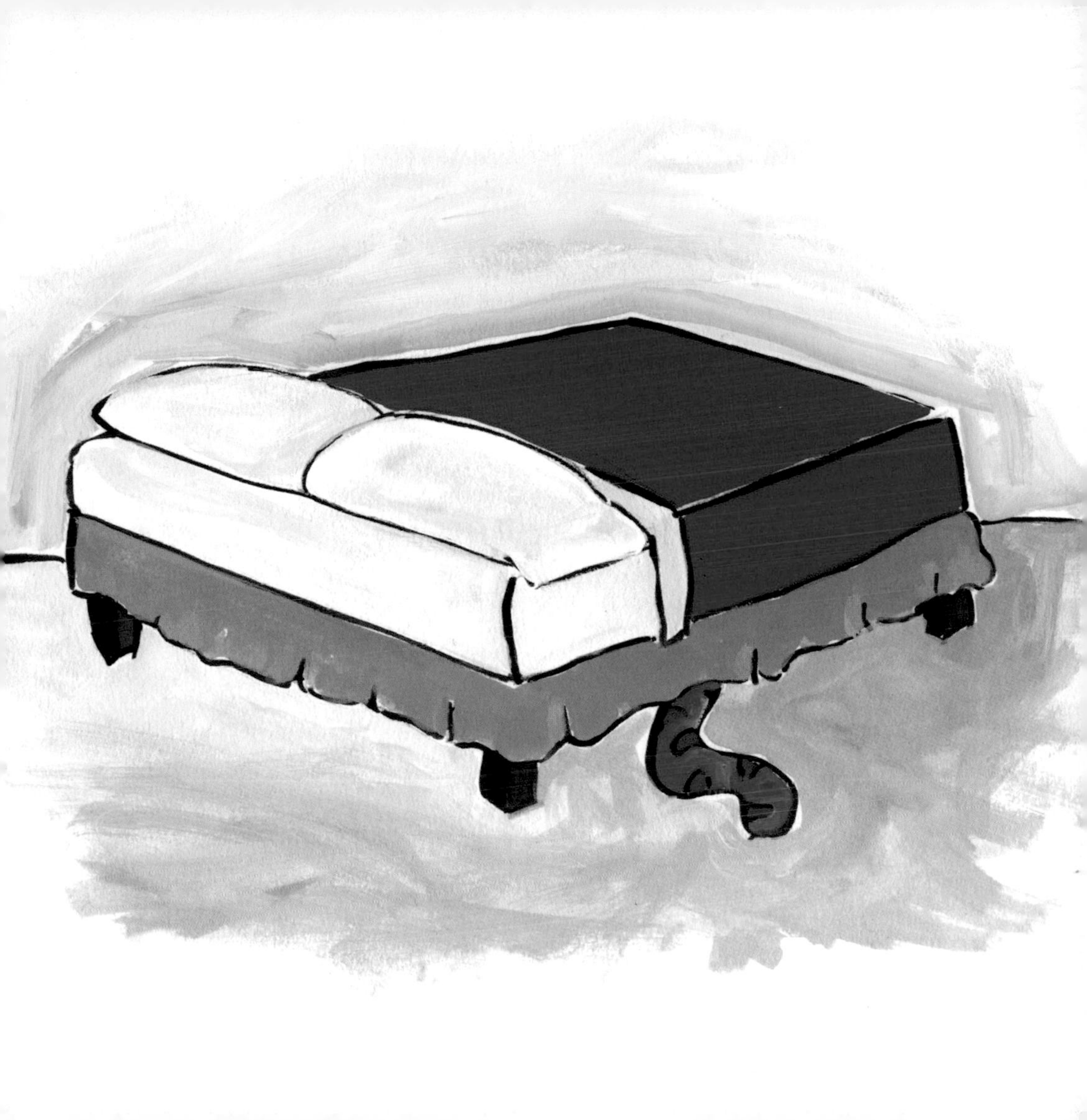

No matter what I'm eating, they want it.

- ☑ Hot Wings
- ☑ Fajitas
- ☑ Lamb Chop
- ☑ Peach Cobbler
- ☑ Chewing Gum
- ☑ Spaghetti-Os
- ☑ Curly Fries
- ☑ Mango
- ☑ Cap'n Crunch with Crunchberries

- ☑ T-Bone
- ☑ Milk Shake
- ☑ BonBons
- ☑ Eggplant
- ☑ Raisinettes
- ☑ Lettuce
- ☑ Whopper
- ☑ Pop Rocks
- ☑ Ding Dongs

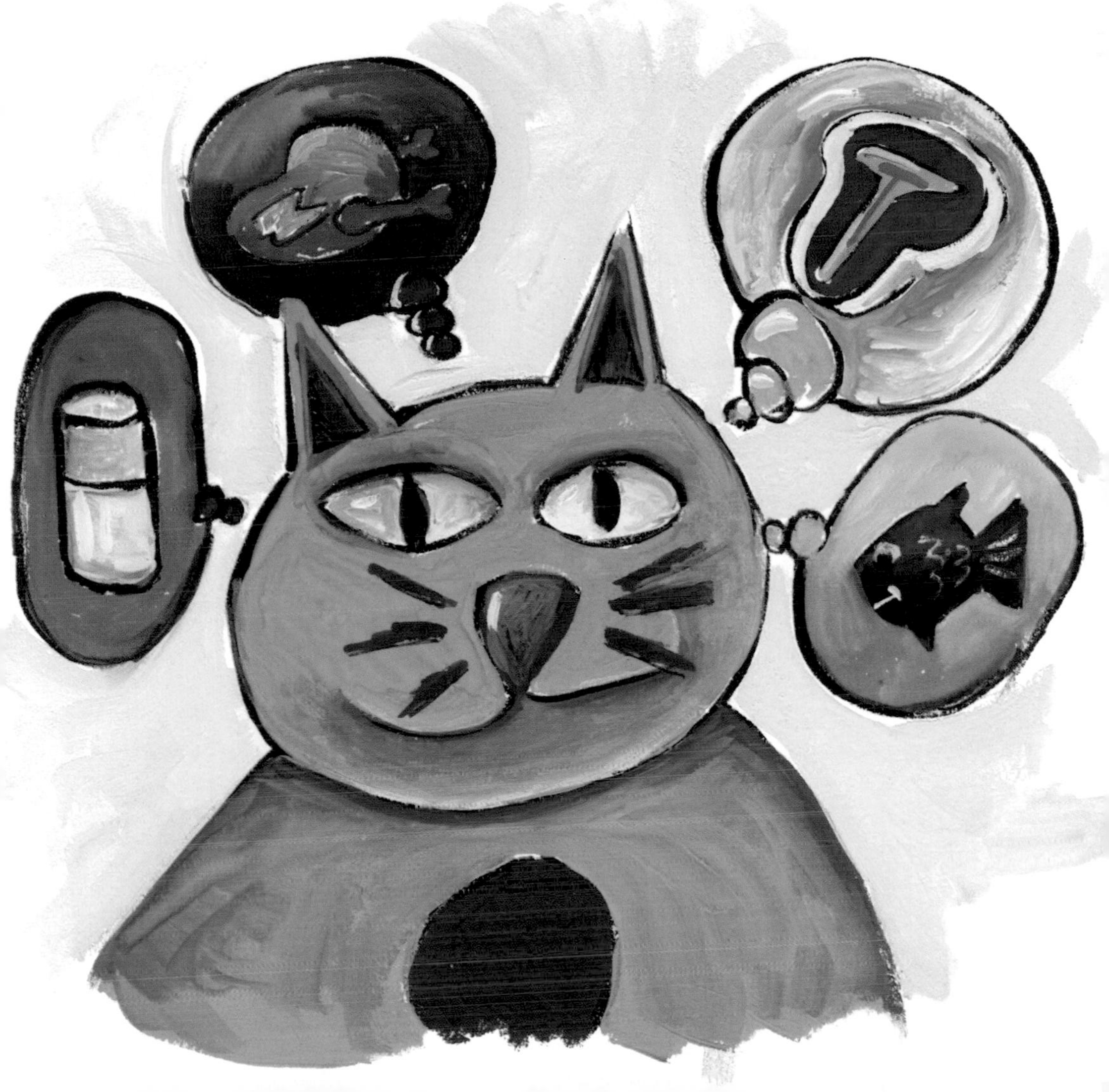

They celebrate the

holidays

in their own

annoying way.

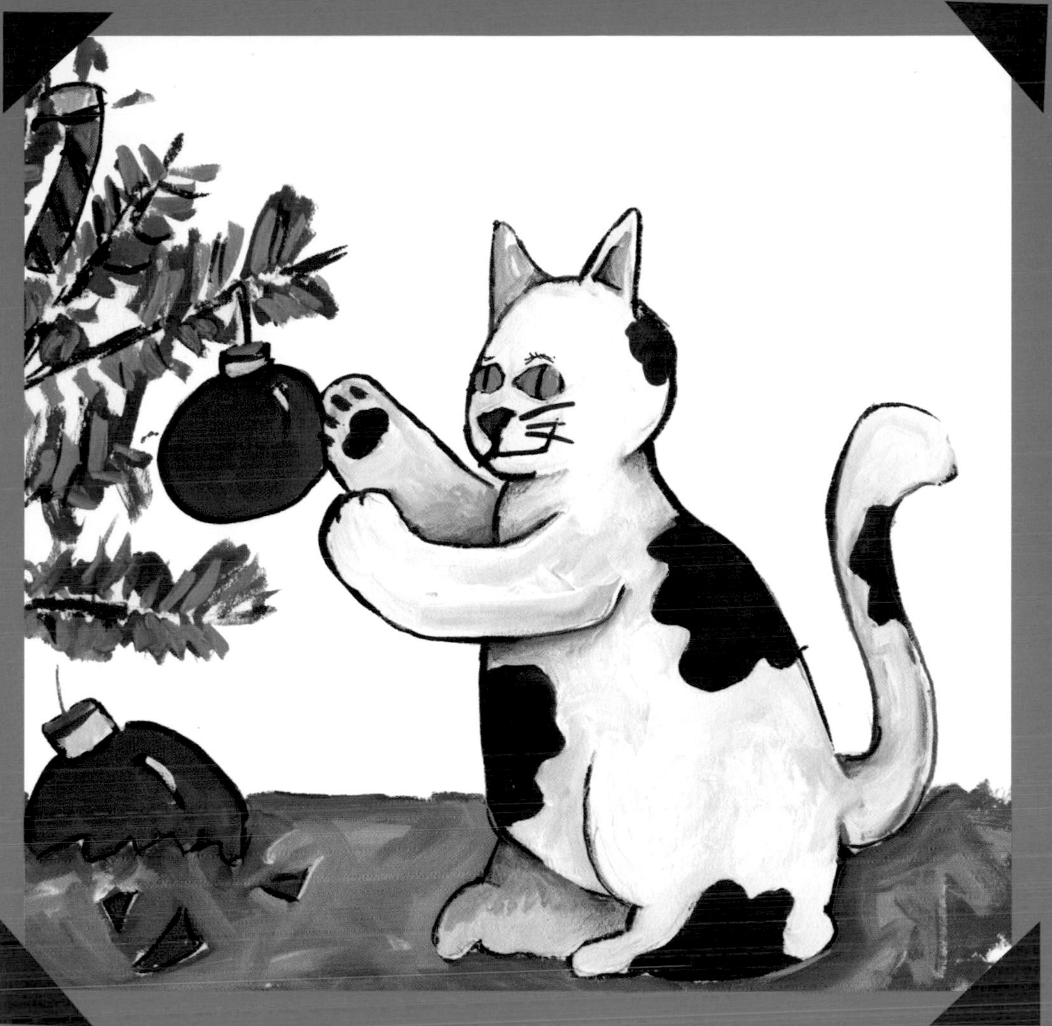

IT'S
ALL
ABOUT
THEM.

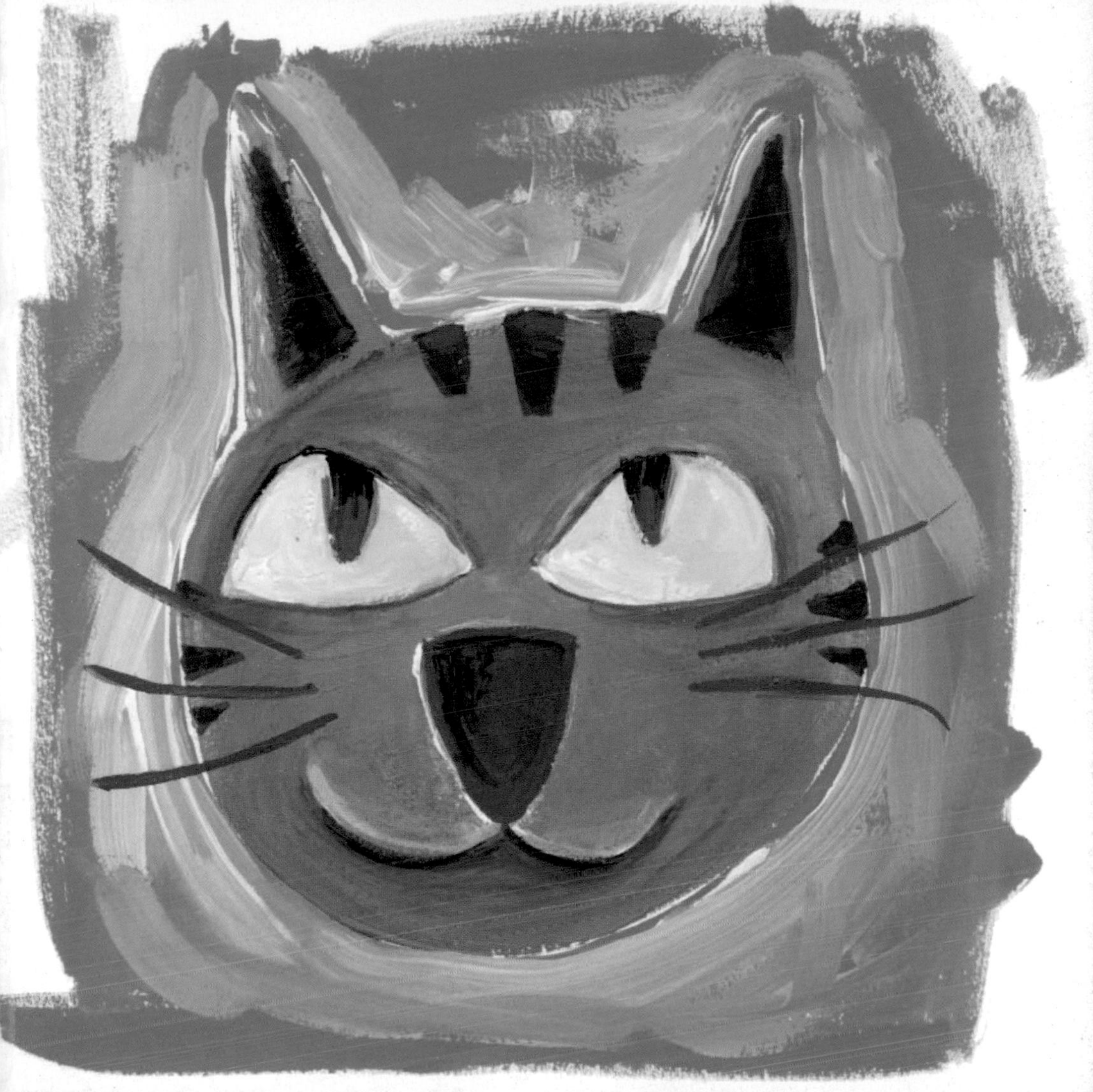

The End!